Beothuk and Micmac

Frank Gouldsmith Speck

BEOTHUK AND MICMAC

PART I

STUDIES OF THE BEOTHUK AND MICMAC OF NEWFOUNDLAND

BY

FRANK G. SPECK

CONTENTS

PART I

PART II

ILLUSTRATIONS

PART I

INDIAN NOTES

I. STUDIES OF THE BEOTHUK AND MICMAC OF NEW-FOUNDLAND

By Frank G. Speck

INTRODUCTION

THE mystery connected with the disappearance of the unfortunate Beothuk or Red Indians of Newfoundland has aroused a great deal of interest among historical investigators. The ethnologist, however, has to lament chiefly the fact that little or nothing of the language or customs of the tribe had been recorded before the opportunity had passed. Paucity of information on the language and the necessity of having to depend on several very poor vocabularies led Powell and Gatschet in 1885 to classify the Beothuk as an independent linguistic stock. Other writers who have dealt with the tribe have been impressed by certain cultural affinities with both Eskimo and Montagnais. Consequently there is at present considerable uncertainty as to the ethnic position of the tribe.

In the summer of 1914, during a trip to the eastern provinces of Canada for ethnological research,[1] I made an extension of my journey, I might almost say a pilgrimage, to Red Indian lake and Exploits river, the country of the Beothuk, in the hope of resurrecting some traditional or material traces of their existence. As a consequence the result of my labor is presented in this brief paper, since in our study of the lost tribe we are forced to make stock of almost any fragments of information. We should be careful, I think, in a case of this kind, not to overestimate the peculiarity of the position of the tribe simply because it became extinct under rather tragic circumstances, or because so little is known of it. Some writers have been inclined to do this. We should rather try to identify the ethnic position of the Beothuk through the few known facts of their life, relying more upon

LOOKOUT TREE AT RED INDIAN POINT

SPECK—BEOTHUK AND MICMAC

VIEW ACROSS RED INDIAN LAKE FROM RED INDIAN POINT, TAKEN FROM NEAR THE TOP
OF "LOOKOUT TREE," SHOWING VIEW OF THE WATER WHERE CARIBOU SWAM BY

positive than upon negative knowledge. The intangible nature of the few existing vocabularies confronts us with our main difficulty; while a few customs, such as the extreme use of red ocher, the peculiar shape of the canoe, and the wigwam pits, features indeed not entirely unknown to outside tribes, tend collectively at least to lend to the Beothuk as an ethnic group a certain aspect of local distinctiveness. Let us glance at the circumstances.

The general supposition that the Beothuk may be a divergent early branch of the eastern Algonkian is indeed borne out by some fairly trustworthy historical, linguistic, and ethnological conclusions. The archeological question is, moreover, correlated with that of the northern New England coast and the maritime provinces. From the reports of Willoughby[2] and Moorehead[3] there is evidence of a pre-Algonkian culture in Maine. It has also been represented that this culture, owing to certain traits, such as the abundant use of red ocher in burials, the absence of many types of stone implements, and the frequent occurrence of long slate lance-heads and of chisels,[4] may have been culture of a type related to that of the Beothuk. While the principle of identifying one type of culture with another on the basis of a few resemblances is, of course, non-commendable, nevertheless the fact that we possess no strikingly conflicting material from either of these little-known ancient areas gives some extra weight to the few resemblances that may be mentioned. At present evidence seems to be accumulating in favor of the idea that a type of culture older and cruder than that of the historic Algonkian prevailed in the eastern maritime provinces and in northern New England. So by coördinating the remainders it might seem that the Beothuk were the last isolated outposts of this culture in the matter of both time and space. Then, if we accept the evidence of Beothuk resemblances to Algonkian as indicating a genetic relationship, we should have to assume that the early culture type belonged to a primitive Algonkian group antedating the later Algonkian occupants. Certain uniformities, one of which is simplicity of type in archeological material throughout the whole area, seem to lead to some such idea. Since a further fundamental simplicity in social, ceremonial, and economic life is a fairly uniform characteristic of the northeastern Algonkian in general, I am inclined to believe that the historic tribes of the northeast are the surviving representatives of the early unaffected Algonkian types of which the isolated Beothuk of Newfoundland were the last true representatives. Unfortunately Mr Howley, in his recent monograph on the Beothuk,[5] does not seem to define clearly the reasons for his own stand on the question of ethnic affinity, notwithstanding the fact that he is at present perhaps more intimately conversant with the internal probabilities of the case than anyone else.[6]

The fame of the Beothuk seems to have reached regions quite distant from Newfoundland in Indian times. As far west as the Penobscot of Maine, a tribe of "Red Indians," who are said to have dyed their skins red, is known by tradition as *Osagane''wi ak*.[7] Some informants apply

this name to the Montagnais of southern
Labrador, while others employ it to designate a people farther to the east, which
makes it possible that they refer to a people
in Newfoundland.

Again, the Malecite of New Brunswick
employ the cognate term *Us'a'gən'ik* to denote the Montagnais and the other tribes to
the north and east. This term is evidently
derived directly from the Micmac term
Osa'γan'ax, which likewise denotes the tribes
north of the St Lawrence as well as the tribe
of Newfoundland. I have found informants to vary on this term, some applying it
to the Montagnais exclusively and others
to the Red Indians of Newfoundland when
they knew something of the latter. We
may remark, however, that a certain stand-
ard usage among the Micmac, Malecite, and
Penobscot applies this term to a people who
may be putatively identified with the Beothuk. In addition, this is the name of the
Beothuk as given by a supposed descendant
of the tribe, born in Newfoundland, whose
testimony will be discussed later.[8]

More definite knowledge of the Beothuk,

or at least those whom we may presume to
be the same, is shared by the Malecite. Under the name of *Me'kwe'isit*, "red man,"
there are several myths and a description
of "a tribe of Indians who were red. Each
of these red men was known by the name of
Me'kwe'isit. Whenever any of the other
Indians came near, these natives would run
away. . . . Their dress was unlike
that of other tribes. They wore a loin cloth
and leggings and moccasins of a peculiar
cut. They did not wear any covering for
the rest of the body, but instead they
painted it a deep red."[9] Mechling, in
commenting on these stories, says: "The
explanation of the Red People suggests
at once the Beothuks. There is little
doubt that they were known to the Malecites
by hearsay at least. The statements in regard to their dress and painting seem to
have some basis in fact."[10] Howley also
gives information from the Malecite obtained through Mr E. Jack, pertaining to
the Beothuk.[11]

Nearer to the scene, the Micmac in general are better acquainted with the former

Red Indians of Newfoundland, who naturally have a prominent place in their local legends. Their name for the Beothuk is *Meɤwe''dji'djik*,[12] "red people" (diminutive), and, as I have said before, the tribal term *Osa'ɤan'ax* is applied by some both to the Montagnais and to the Beothuk by the present-day Newfoundland Indians.

Among the Montagnais, on the other hand, I have had very poor success in obtaining references to the Beothuk. As far down the St Lawrence as the Moisie river the Montagnais seem ignorant of the Newfoundland tribe's existence. Farther east, nearer the Straits of Belle Isle, perhaps the few Montagnais there would know something of them, but I have not as yet visited them to determine the point.

The expectation that the present Micmac inhabitants of Newfoundland might have a more extended knowledge of the supposedly extinct tribe, an expectation most natural to the ethnologist, led me to undertake the investigation of material culture while in Newfoundland, the results of which form the basis of this paper. The ethnological

RED INDIAN POINT, RED INDIAN LAKE, SHOWING "LOOKOUT TREE" AND BEACH,
LOOKING SOUTH

THE SAME SCENE AS THAT SHOWN IN PLATE III. LOOKING TOWARD MARY MARCH
BEND AND POINT

collection figured in my study is now in the Victoria Museum, Ottawa, and the manuscript was prepared originally for the Anthropological Survey of Canada. Thanks are due to the Director and to Dr. Edward Sapir for the photographs of the collection and for permission to use the material.

SITES OF BEOTHUK OCCUPANCY

In the neighborhood of Red Indian lake and the River of Exploits the signs of Beothuk occupancy are both numerous and well preserved. Several authors[13] have written of the caribou "fences" which were constructed to force the caribou to cross a river or a lake at certain places accessible to the natives, where they could be shot and speared.[14] Recent forest fires have obliterated these so-called "fences," but in a few places near the shore, where, on account of the moisture, the fires have not burned to the water's edge, some few miles below the new dam on Exploits river at its junction with Red Indian lake, are to be seen the trunks of trees felled to form a line barrier leading obliquely from the water's edge to the wooded bank. This rough abattis, as it were, is said to have extended for some miles along the river before the era of fires which wrought so much havoc with the forests of the interior. So well known are the sites of these fences in the Exploits River region that any Micmac guide at Badger's Brook can lead to the places where remains may still be seen. At one spot in particular, a mile above Red Indian falls on Exploits river, a "fence" running to the water's edge is discernible. It is formed of cross-pieces as high as one's head, with horizontal tree-trunks felled to fall into the crotches here and there. The continuation of this "fence" has been burnt away upon the upland, but it is still partly intact along shore.

During the short time at my disposal, I was able to find without difficulty several interesting camp-sites where even the form of the wigwam-sites was preserved and some of the litter of the hunter's camp lay round about near the surface. One of the noteworthy features of the Red Indian sites is the excavation of the ground where the wigwams stood. Either circular or somewhat quadrilateral in form, these pits now generally appear excavated about a foot. They were undoubtedly deeper when made. In the center of the wigwam-holes is the location of the fireplace, as indicated by the charred soil and fire-cracked stones. Digging over the soil around the fireplaces one uncovers remains of implements. Chert and flint chips occur, showing stone-age industry. Interspersed with them were found metal fragments—pieces of metal bands, old wrought nails, small nondescript iron scraps, and, in one place, a perfect iron awl blade. Quantities of animal bones and pieces of caribou antler also occur, indicating the food habits of the natives. Referring to the material, we find a tradition among the Micmac-Montagnais of the island which relates how the Red Indians used to make forays on fishermen's settlements and even robbed schooners to obtain metal for tool making.[15] The Micmac say that they frequently dig in these Red Indian wigwam-pits and find curious iron implements—knives, axes, traps, and the like.

At Red Indian point, several miles south of Millertown at the point of land near where Mary March brook flows into the lake, is a notable site, said by the Micmac-Montagnais to have been the headquarters of the Red Indians a hundred years or so ago. Directly at the point here are a number of wigwam-pits, at least seven, although it was rather hard to discern them all at the time of my visit on account of the logs that had drifted in and filled the pits at high water. One of these, rectangular in shape and about 30 feet in its greater diameter, is said to have been the location of the wigwam of a chief. The other pits are at several yards' distance, grouped around this one. They have an average depth of about 2 feet, and their large size indicates the place formerly to have been a large and probably more or less regular settlement. In and around these pits I gathered a quantity of cracked bones and pieces of antler. Much material undoubtedly could be obtained here by excavation. The

"MARY MARCH'S TREE" AT MARY MARCH POINT. NEAR MILLERTOWN.
NEWFOUNDLAND.

The tree is said to have been that under which Mary March was taken captive in 1819

BEOTHUK WIGWAM PIT AT JUNCTION OF BADGER'S BROOK AND EXPLOITS RIVER

Stones have been placed to indicate the margin of the pit

most interesting feature of this site, however, is a large white spruce tree which
stands intact at the extremity of the point.
This tree has its smaller branches trimmed
out, and the lower branches are lopped off
a foot or so from the trunk to form a means
of ascent to its airy heights. The trimming
extends, I should say, at least 30 or 40 feet
from the ground, and enables an observer
to mount conveniently the full distance.
This tree was a lookout post. When the
camp was occupied a lookout was stationed
in it to watch for caribou swimming across
the lake, or, we might well imagine, for the
approach of enemies. This remarkable tree
is still in perfect condition and forms a
landmark that seems to have appealed to
the sentiment of the lumbermen, so it will
probably remain. Photographs of this
site, and several views of the lookout tree,
one taken from its height where I climbed to
experience the sensation of observing these
wastes from the vantage point of the ancients, are shown in pl. I-V. One fact
further should be noted, that in the last
century the point was occupied by Micmac

who availed themselves from time to time of its ideal situation. John Paul said that he knew of several old people who were born while their families were encamped there. Among them he mentioned it as his understanding that Santu, the woman whose claim of Beothuk descent is to be considered later, was also born there.

At many points on Exploits river, the wigwam-pits are numerous. Near the junction of Badger's brook and Exploits river, the only other place where I had an opportunity to examine the shores, about a dozen wigwam-pits may still be seen ranging along the northern bank on the terrace above the beach. On some of these pits, fair-sized spruce trees have grown up. The pits are situated at a distance ranging from about 100 feet to 100 yards from each other (pl. VI). In some of these, where I excavated the fireplace and floor space, fragments of iron tools, stone chips and flakes, and stone hammers or bone-crackers, and a perfect bone implement for removing the hair from caribou skins, were found. The latter, a caribou leg-bone, is of the same type as is commonly found among the Montagnais, Micmac, and other eastern tribes. (See pl. XXV, *a*, *b*). So much for the archeological remains of which I am able to speak from personal observation. The Micmac of the region, however, speak of many of these old camp-sites. Some systematic excavation in the region would prove very profitable.

THE MICMAC AND THE RED INDIANS

Our most important extant sources of information about the Beothuk are undoubtedly the Micmac-Montagnais who still inhabit the southern and western coasts of Newfoundland and parts of the interior. The present Indian inhabitants, whose language is Micmac, are the mixed offspring of Montagnais hunters from Labrador and Micmac from Cape Breton island. Immigration from both these neighboring regions must have commenced at least several centuries ago, because our records from the early part of the nineteenth century show both the Micmac and the Montagnais to have been firmly established in Newfoundland at that time. As the historical facts concerned with these migrations are quite interesting, a brief account of them will be given to introduce the people we are to discuss as the successors, I believe in more than one sense, of the Beothuk.[16]

The Micmac claim to have had some knowledge of Newfoundland from remote times. They speak of a branch of their people called *Sa·'ɣəwe·djki·k*, "ancients," who lived on the southern and western coasts before the eighteenth century, and to corroborate this they give an old nomenclature of landmarks in various parts of the island in Micmac. Communication with Newfoundland in early times was carried on by means of canoes. The distance, about 93 miles, between Cape North (of Cape Breton) and Cape Ray was covered in two stages, the first stop having been St Paul's island, 14 miles from Cape North. The traverse thence was made at night generally, when it was calmer, guided by a beacon fire kindled on the high barrens of Cape Ray by a crew of experienced men who went on rapidly ahead of the main body. In later times the Micmac added to the facility of communication by using schooners. Their first settlements were about St George's bay, at Burgeo on the south coast, and at Conne river.

In the St George's Bay region it is a matter of general knowledge, among the older members of the Newfoundland band, that their ancestors lived in amicable contact with the Beothuk, whom they designate *Meɣwe''djik,* "red people." This period of friendly relationship interests us now because during that time we may surmise some culture borrowing and blood intermixture to have taken place.

The following legend narrated by John Paul accounts for the rupture between the two tribes.

How the Micmac and the Red Indians Became Separated
(Narrated by John Paul at Badger's Brook)

"Long ago the Micmac and the Red Indians were friendly and lived together in a village at St George's bay, which is now supposed to have been near Seal rocks [near Stevensville]. The place was called *Meski'gluwi''dən,* 'big gut,' or it might have been *Nudjo'ɣɑn,* inside Sandy point in the bay. The St George's river was at that time called Main river by the English. Everything went well between the two tribes. They used to have a large canoe at the village in which the people could cross over the bay.   One time during the winter a Micmac boy killed a black weasel. As it was winter-time the weasel should, of course, have been white.   The occurrence was taken as an omen of misfortune,[17] because the boy should not have killed a black weasel in winter-time, the animal not being in its proper hue.   On account of the violation of the taboo a quarrel arose between the boys who were at the time gathered near the big canoe already mentioned.   The Micmac boy struck and killed a Red Indian boy and left him there. Soon the Red Indian boy was missed by his people, and after searching for several days they found his body lying near the big canoe. When they examined the wounds the Red Indians concluded that the boy had been murdered.   They accused the Micmac of doing the deed, and in a few days feeling became so intense that a fight ensued in which the Red Indians were beaten and driven out.   They retreated into the interior and, being separated from contact with the outside world, drifted into barbarism and became wilder.   They always shunned the Micmac, who soon after obtained firearms and, although they never persecuted the Red Indians, were thenceforth objects of terror to them.   In a few generations those of the two tribes who were able to converse together died out and there was no way left for them to come together.   So living in fear of each other, yet avoiding clashes, the Micmac continued to live at Bay St George and the Red Indians kept to the interior."

We can hardly give serious historical consideration to the details of this story. It bears the marks of being a secondary explanation of some historical event, especially since the same general theme among the Micmac, and even among other Wabanaki tribes of the mainland, accounts for the hostility of the Iroquois.[18]   The motive of the legend, nevertheless, is clear enough, for it indicates that the Micmac and the Red Indians were undoubtedly on friendly terms originally and that they intermingled.[19]

Accepting this assumption as being trustworthy, let us consider other claims, as well as some features of material culture. Such a study of the ethnology of the Newfoundland Indians (whom I have chosen to call Micmac-Montagnais on account of their mixed descent), as I was able to make it in the early summer of 1914, showed some few articles of use characteristic neither of the Micmac of the mainland nor of the Montagnais.   By eliminating what we can safely attribute to either of the above sources, the residual material may possibly deserve to be classed as the result of borrowing through contact with the Beothuk. If one is inclined to object strenuously to such a claim, let us recall the fact that many of the Micmac families among the present-day natives of Newfoundland are of Montagnais descent. If one attempts to deny categorically that culture survivals from the Beothuk are not to be traced through the Micmac, on account of former hostility, then it cannot be denied on the same ground that influence could have come down through the Montagnais strain in the present population, whose ancestors were known to be friendly with the Beothuk.

COMPARATIVE ETHNOLOGICAL NOTES

One of the distinctive features of economic life listed for the Beothuk is a marked peculiarity in the construction of the birch-bark wigwam. The excavation of a pit a foot or so below the level of the ground seems to have been a general feature of the Beothuk wigwam. This contrasts with the Micmac

LOG WIGWAM, CAMP OF FRANK JOE AND FAMILY NEAR ST GEORGE'S BAY

ANOTHER VIEW OF WIGWAM CONSTRUCTION

and Montagnais wigwam, because these tribes generally erect the wigwam upon flat ground. On the Penobscot river in Maine, nevertheless, such wigwam-pits, both rectangular and circular in outline, may be seen on Indian island. In other respects, however, the wigwams of the Beothuk and the eastern Algonkian seem to correspond even in such details as the hoop encircling the inside of the framework of poles.[20] The hoop varies somewhat in size according to the height at which it is placed. Generally it is lashed to the wigwam poles about six feet from the ground and lends much to the support of the poles when the wigwam is burdened with snow. Sticks are placed on the hoop, upon which clothing and moccasins may be hung to be dried. Even the cooking utensils are suspended over the fire from the cross-sticks. All is shown in pl. XL. The hoop as a structural feature, is used, we know, westward as far as the Montagnais and the Penobscot of Maine;[21] but it is absent from the wigwam and tipi construction of the Great Lakes area and the plains. Even the rectangular based winter

wigwams of the Beothuk, built of logs chink-
ed with moss and with a pyramidal bark
superstructure, find their parallel among
the tribes of the Wabanaki group. An example of the present-day Newfoundland Indian log camp is shown in pl. VII–VIII. An
anonymous author in the London *Times*
(1820) mentions the upright posts in construction (cf. Howley, p. 100). This camp
is built partly on the same principle—a clear
survival. So after all, in the rather fundamental matter of architecture the Beothuk do not exhibit a great divergence from
the surrounding Algonkian.

In canoe-building we find another important subject for comparative mention. The
bark canoe of the Beothuk type has
been described by several authors.[22] The
pointed keel and the elevated middle section
of the gunwales are the two distinguishing
features of the craft. The pointed keel is
unique among eastern canoe types, but the
same cannot be said of the elevated gunwale
middle, for a modified form of the same
thing, with the same separating thwart, is
prominent not only in the Micmac canoes

BIRCH-BARK CANOES USED BY THE MICMAC OF THE NEW BRUNSWICK COAST, SHOWING THE
FEATURE OF THE ELEVATED GUNWALE CENTERS, CALLED "HUMPBACKS"

Photograph by Dr W. D. Wallis

a

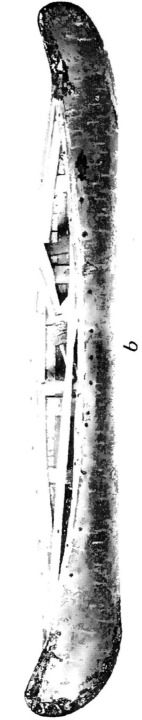

b

CANOES OF THE BADGER'S BROOK BAND OF MICMAC

a, Model of caribou-skin canoe. *b*, Model of birch-bark canoe. Note thwarts and peaked gunwale,
features possibly borrowed from the Beothuk

of Newfoundland (pl. IX, *b*), which might be expected to show the feature, but throughout the Micmac range as far as southern Nova Scotia, according to my own observation (pl. IX). Farther west than the Micmac, however, this feature does not extend nor do the Montagnais produce it. Ordinarily, however, the present-day Micmac-Montagnais of Newfoundland make and use the moose-skin canoe (*mu'sœwulk*, "moose boat") in preference to the bark one. They claim that it is more convenient on the portages and more quickly made. From two to four skins are used in its construction, which is quite simple. A model is shown in pl. X, *a*. In this trait the Newfoundland Indians agree with the other tribes of the Wabanaki group, as well as with the Montagnais, who all have recourse at times to moose-hide craft. We do not hear of the hide canoe among the Beothuk from any of the old accounts with the exception of one, Cormack's,[23] although of course the fundamental idea is Eskimo as well as Algonkian.

In the matter of dress, some articles are

characteristic of the Newfoundland Indians of today which are common to both Montagnais and Micmac, while others are suggestive of Red Indian culture. The caribou-skin capote (*qali'bua''zi*, "caribou covering") with hood attached (pl. XI–XIV), and the sealskin coats (pl. XV) of the same type, are of course in the former class. Although I was able to procure only a plain specimen of the caribou-skin coat, I learned from John Paul (see p. 78, note 45) of decorations which formerly were more common. Tanned with the hair off, these coats had figures of animals painted on the back, and a band of checkerwork in red and black around the waist. This compares more with what we know of Montagnais decoration, although the same type of coat had a wide distribution throughout the Wabanaki area. Of the pigments, réd and brown were from alder bark, yellow from "yellow thread" (golden thread, *Coptis trifolia*),[24] and blue and black from blueberries. When the hair was left on these coats they were seldom painted, except as in the case of the one figured, which has red ocher

DAUGHTER OF JOHN PAUL, MICMAC-MONTAGNAIS OF
BADGER'S BROOK, IN CARIBOU-SKIN COAT

smeared over the seams on the inside. Children's coats were made from the skin of a caribou calf, with the eye-holes and ears left in place on the head, which fitted over the head of the child to form the hood. This is distinctly like the coats worn by children of the Montagnais of Labrador. Trousers of tanned caribou-skin reaching almost to the knee, as an article of clothing correspond also to the early dress of the Montagnais.

The women wore peaked caps (*kon'ī'-skwe'tc*, "pointed top"), descriptions of which serve to show that they were more like those of the other Micmac, though of course a similar article is worn by nearly every Montagnais woman. The women also wrapped their hair over two small wooden blocks over the ears, also after the fashion of the Montagnais. Neither of these fashions, however, is to be seen nowadays (pl. XVI–XVII).

When we come to consider boots and moccasins (*mkī'zi'n*), we encounter articles which evidently suggest Beothuk influence. The low moccasin of caribou-skin has the forepart finely puckered like that of the

Montagnais (pl. XVIII, *a*, *b*). More characteristic of these Indians, however, is the boot-moccasin (*mu'ksan*),[25] the pattern of which is the same as that of Eskimo boots and those of the Montagnais of the coast. With feet made of sealskin and the upper parts of either seal- or caribou-skin, heavily greased, the article is suggestively Eskimo-like. Frequently the top of the boot is reinforced with a strip of caribou-skin with the fur on (pl. XVIII, *c–e*). The distinctive feature of both the moccasin and the boots, however, is the red stain which they receive at the hands of their makers before being considered complete. Discussion of this peculiarity with the Indians themselves brought to light the fact that they attribute the custom of dyeing these articles red to former contact with the Red Indians. Since the feature seems to be restricted to those people, I see little reason to doubt the likelihood of the connection. Practically every pair of moccasins I observed worn by them was dyed red, whether made of caribou-skin or of seal-skin. To obtain the red color they soak the hide in water im-

AUGHTER OF JOHN PAUL, MICMAC-MONTAGNAIS (
BADGER'S BROOK, IN CARIBOU-SKIN COAT

MAN'S COAT OF CARIBOU-SKIN WITH THE HAIR ON AND
WITH BUTTONS OF CARIBOU-ANTLER; USED IN WINTER
BY THE BADGER'S BROOK BAND OF MICMAC

pregnated with spruce, pine
during the process of tanni

For a people with rather
it seems unusual to find
weaving. Upon a loom (*elda*
ing instrument''[27]) made of
20 to 30 holes in the bars
tical apertures (pl. XIX), th
pack-straps (*wi'sxə''buxs*
strap''), shown in pl. XX, *a, b;*
the Cape Breton dialect
xada'u) belts and garters.[2]
employed in weaving, before
into use, was caribou wool
wool it was combed from
fourths of a pound usually
skin. Bear, beaver, otter,
they say, also furnished wo
sort. When combed and st
was spun on a wooden s[
da'ɣan', ''spinning instrume
twirled with the fingers (pl.
resting on a board. When tl
are ready to be woven, t
alternately through the h
the loom. One end of the g

strands is tied to a post, or something equally convenient in the house, and the other end attached to the belt of the woman who is to do the weaving. Thus the loom is near the body of the weaver. By leaning backward then the weaver can make the cords as tight as she desires. Without shuttle or bar the weaver then passes the ball of yarn with one hand between the alternate strands, separated vertically when the loom is raised with the other hand, and then back again when the loom is lowered. This produces an over-one under-one mesh, and the pattern is determined by the colors of the strands. Pl. xix shows the loom with an unfinished belt upon it. The art of weaving, the highest artistic accomplishment of the Newfoundland band, seems more closely related to the Micmac; nothing like it occurs among the Montagnais. Several informants claimed, however, that they had heard of its derivation from the Red Indians. I hardly think, though, that such a claim should be seriously considered.

Another rather fine art is the weaving of very fine cords of rabbit wool in varied

MICMAC-MONTAGNAIS WOMAN AT BADGER'S BROOK
SEALSKIN CAPOTE WITH SNOWSHOES OF LOCAL TYPE

FRANK JOE AND WIFE, MICMAC-MONTAGNAIS OF ST
GEORGE'S BAY SETTLEMENT, WEST COAST OF
NEWFOUNDLAND

colors to be sewed on the edge of caps, cloth
ing, and the like, sometimes made int
designs as a substitute for beadwork an
painting. This art is comparable with th
former work of the Montagnais in woc
embroidery, and in later days in silk.
have described this technique in anothe
paper.[30]

The scarcity of skin and cloth bags amon
the Newfoundland Indians contrasts wit
their abundance among the Montagnai
and even the Micmac of the mainland
Only a few bags or pouches (*malsewi'*[31]
were obtained (pl. XXII), one of caribou
skin, dyed red, and another of muskrat
skin.

Snowshoes (*a'ɣɔmk'*), shown in pl. XXIII
are not so finely made as are those c
the Montagnais. They resemble more th
snowshoes of the Micmac of the mainland.
Crooked knives (*waɣa'ɣan*); awls wit
wooden handles (*sisi''gan*); hide-scraper
and hair-removers (*saɣwi''gan*); snowsho
needles (*tatwi''gan*) of caribou antler o
bone; netting needles (*sa''ɣadik'*) of woo
(all shown in pl. XXIV–XXVII), are all of

type common to both the Montagnais and the Micmac.[33] There is no reason why many of them should not have been the same among the Beothuk, since one hair-remover at least of the common sort was found, as I have previously mentioned, in a Beothuk wigwam pit at Badger's Brook (pl. VI). There is, however, nothing distinctive in any way about implements of the class described,

FIG. 1.—Leaf of *Sarracena purpurea* (pitcher plant) used as an improvised pipe by Newfoundland Indians.

for the types are present among all the tribes of the northeastern culture group.

Harpoon-heads of antler are represented in the collection by several types, one for spearing beaver (*sumuskwa'ndï*) shown in pl. XXVIII, *e*; others for seals and caribou (*a, c*). The antler toggle (*d*) is called *pska'o*.[34] These lances and harpoons, and the fish-spear (*ni·γo'γɔl;* pl. XXVIII, *b*), are also of the type common among the Eskimo, Mon-

WIFE OF FRANK JOE WEARING CHARACTERISTIC HEAD-
COVERING

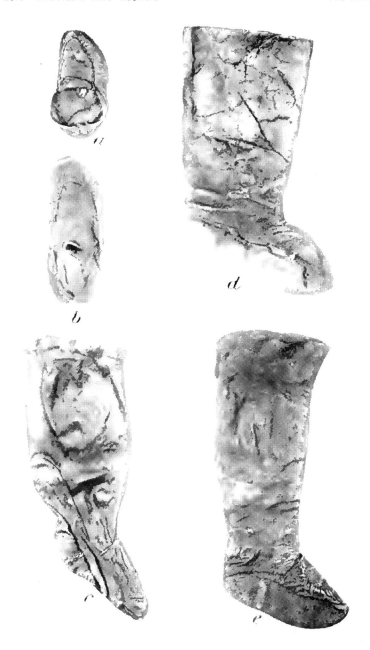

BOOTS AND MOCCASINS OF THE BADGER'S BROOK BAND OF MICMAC

a, Child's red tanned sealskin moccasin. *b*, Man's red tanned caribou-skin moccasin. *c*, Boot of sealskin with caribou-fur trimming. *d*, Boot with upper of tanned sealskin and feet of caribou-skin (length, 14 in.). *e*, Red tanned caribou-skin top boot moccasins

tagnais, and Micmac; in fact, throughout the North.

Smoking-pipes are improvised from the leaf of the pitcher-plant (*Sarracena purpurea*), shown in fig. 1. The green tubular leaf body endures for a period long enough for the user to enjoy one filling of it, either with tobacco or with dried red-willow bark. The natives also use an improvised pipe made of a roll of birch-bark. Howley (p. 339) mentions the same smoking materials and adds that they were probably used also by the Beothuk.

Maple splint baskets (*pudali'e'wi*,[35] pl. XXIX) are the comparatively recent products of an art brought from the Micmac of the mainland, for nothing of the kind is found among the Montagnais, nor in fact was it found in earlier times among any of the other Wabanaki.[36] On the other hand, the decorated birch-bark baskets so characteristic of the Montagnais are not common in Newfoundland either, and we find only a few of the beautiful quillworked bark boxes of the Micmac type. Since porcupines are not native to Newfoundland, the few old

FIG. 2—Wooden dipper for molten lead in making bullets

women who, a generation ago, preserved the national art of quillwork on bark (pl. XXX) had to import their quills from Nova Scotia. Bark boxes are *a'luwabax*, "oval shaped;" and *awiꞏyo'ɣalaɣan*, "round bark box." They were formerly common objects.[37]

From several hunters I obtained perforated stones (*kwunde'u*, "stone;" pl. XXXI, *b*, *c*) which they cherished as luck charms to aid them in hunting. Neither among the Montagnais nor the Micmac, so far, have I encountered the same fetishes, although I had obtained them previously from the Penobscot of Maine.

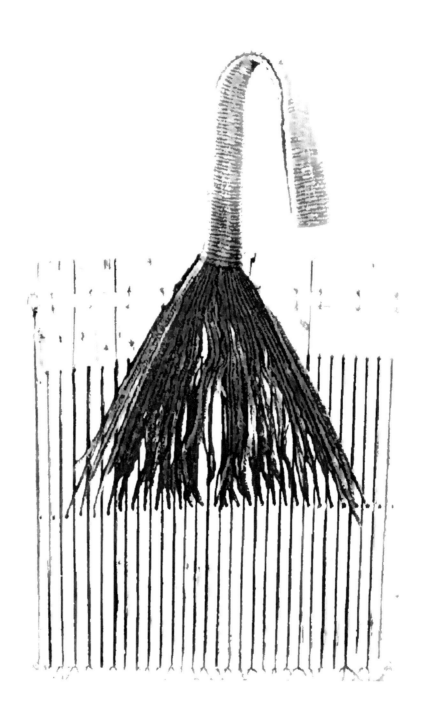

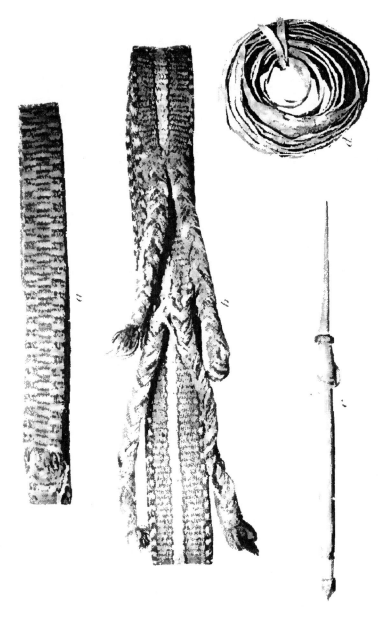

WOVEN PACK-STRAPS, AND SPINDLE-WHORL

a, b, d, Pack-straps of the Badger's Brook band of Micmac. *c,* Spindle-whorl
from St. George's bay

Should these be also considered as Beothuk borrowings, they are at least of an Algonkian nature. A luck charm consisting of seven lynx teeth attached to a cord was obtained from a hunter of the Badger's Brook band. Among all the northern tribes similar fetish objects are in fashion. Animals' teeth perforated for suspension have also been found in Beothuk graves.[38]

To conclude this brief account of Newfoundland material culture I might add a few notes on Beothuk ethnology, giving some of the ideas possessed by the present Micmac of the island (see pl. xxxii). "The Red Indian canoes were made of bark, shaped like a 'bean' and pointed at the bottom. They were very ticklish, but the Red Indians could manage them perfectly. They wore caribou-skin clothes with the fur turned inside or tanned, and lined with otter, beaver, or other kinds of fur. They were not so much characterized by having their clothing dyed red as their skin. They wore hooded coats, frequently decorated with painting, pants and boots."[39]

A small collection of ethnological objects,

which my own collection duplicates, obtained from the present-day Indians of the island, is in the Museum of the Geological Survey of Newfoundland, having been collected years ago by Mr Howley. They are of the same type as those just described. A more important collection of stone implements from many parts of the coast and from the Exploits region is also to be seen there. Some of the bone and antler implements and the birch-bark receptacles are of the same type as those which I have just discussed as being common among the Algonkian of the East in general. One cannot escape the impression again that the Beothuk articles in this collection are of a distinctly Algonkian character.

Gatschet's idea[40] that the Beothuk differed from most other Indians in being of a lighter color, in having the excavations in their lodges for sleeping-berths, in the form of their canoes, in the non-domestication of the dog,[41] and the absence of pottery, of course, is not of great importance, because most of these remarks would apply to the ethnology of some of the neighboring tribes.

TABLE OF ETHNOLOGICAL COMPARISONS

Beothuk	Micmac-Montagnais (Newfoundland)	Micmac (Maritime Provinces)	Montagnais (Labrador)
Use of red ocher on clothing, body, utensils etc	Red dye on footwear, bags		Red ocher occas[ional] utensils, games,
Conical bark wigwam with hoop How ley pp 29-30	Similar	Similar	Bark and skin wi[th] hoops occasiona[l]
Rectangular wigwam with upright post (Howley pp 100 211) and bark super structure	Similar	Rectangular log wigwam bark super structure	Rectangula, kind wam of his sometst[ructure]
Excavated wigwam late circular and rectangular (Howley pp 85-345)		Slight wigwam excavation Le Clercq p 101	
Bark canoe elevated gunwale centre pointed bottom (Howley pp 31-32 271 pl XXXI XXXII) Skin canoes (Howley pp 152-213)	Skin canoe and bark canoe elevated gunwale center	Similar	Skin can[oe] and [bark] elevated rail
Hooded deerskin coats with or without sleeves (Howley p 212)	Hooded deerskin coats with sleeves	Coats Robes with detached sleeves (Denys p 412 Le Clercq p 93)	Dressed coats s[kin] without sleeve and [...]
Caribou hock boot (Howley pp 271-322)	Similar	Moose hock boot	M[oose] and ca[ribou]
Women's tuques ?	Tuque and pointed cap	Pointed cap	R[ou]nded tuque
Deer fence (Howley pp 69-70 157)			Deer fence
Rather long netted snowshoes (Howley p 87)	Similar	Similar	Broad netted [...]
Reinforced bow (Howley p 271)			
Antler and bone harpoons scrapers arrows needles etc	Similar	Antler and bone harpoons Denys p 420 scrapers nee[dles] Le Denys pp 406-415	Antler and bone sc[ra]pers knives, a[...] this
(?)	Woven wool pack straps and belts	Leather pack straps	Braided leather straps bark pack straps
Birch bark vessels and receptacles (Howley pl XXXIV p 249)	Similar	Similar	Similar
Seal stomach oil receptacle (Howley p 246, sketches VI VII)	Similar		Seal stomach grea[se rece]ptacle
Baby sack (no mention of cradle board	Baby sack	Cradle board also Denys p 403 Le Clercq p 89	Baby sack
Bone dress ornaments ? (Howley pl XXV-XXVIII)			
Throwing-dice game (Howley pl XXV-XXVIII)	Throwing dice game	Throwing-dice and dice and bowl game	
Bird skulls and animals teeth as fetishes (Howley pp 331-340 pl XXV)	Mammals' skulls preserved as fetishes	Similar also Le Clercq p 226	Wild fowl and m[...] preserved as feti[shes]
Series of triangles chief motive in decorative engraving (Howley, pl XXXV-XXXVIII)	Series of triangles in wood carving	Geometrical figures in etching on birch bark. Series of triangles in wood carving	Geometrical figures on birch bark triangles in woo[d]
Decapitation of enemies (Howley, p 282 et passim and p 180)		Similar (also scalping, Le Clercq p 270	Similar
Burials in birch bark covering Howley p 214)		Corpse wrapped in birch bark on staging later buried in bark coffin (Denys pp 438-39) interment in bark covering (LeClercq p 301) on scaffold in water (p 301)	Tree burials in coffin

MICMAC-MONTAGNAIS AT BADGER'S BROOK, SHOWING METHOD OF USING WOVEN PACK-STRAP

a

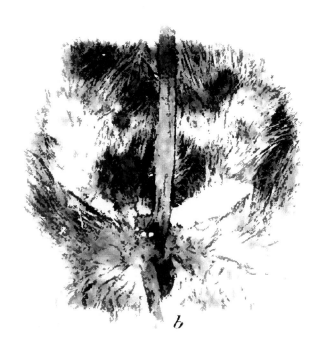

b

TOBACCO-POUCHES OF THE BADGER'S BROOK BAND OF
MICMAC

a, Of red tanned caribou-skin, with string of spun caribou wool; width,
4½ in. *b*, Of muskrat-skin

Moreover, the isolated fact that the Beothuk used the inner bark of *Pinus balsamifera* for food[42] is, like many other customs, not an exclusive one, because the Montagnais do the same with the inner rind of canoe birch when pressed by famine.

The accompanying tabulated ethnological summary has been prepared for the convenience of the reader. It reveals, on the basis of what is known of Beothuk ethnology, the degree of resemblance of the Beothuk to the Micmac-Montagnais of Newfoundland, and that of these two peoples individually to the Montagnais north of the St Lawrence and to the Micmac and the Wabanaki tribes south of that stream. A tabulation of this nature is of course valuable only to a limited extent, because we cannot rely on the significance of anything negative owing to the incompleteness of our knowledge of the Beothuk. As for the other tribes in the columns, since the list is not intended to focus their characteristics as a body apart from those of the Beothuk, the significance of the comparison is even less, for its scope is restricted to the Beothuk correspondences. The blank spaces in the columns denote that the particular feature is lacking, so far as the data show. The references in the Beothuk column are to Howley's monograph; the statements referring to the other tribes are based mostly on my own field observations. The other authorities, where mentioned, are: Nicholas Denys, The Description and Natural History of the Coasts of North America . . . Paris, 1672, reprinted in Publications of the Champlain Society, Toronto, 1908, by W. F. Ganong; and Father Chrestien Le Clercq, New Relation of Gaspesia . . . Paris, 1691, reprinted in Publications of the Champlain Society, Toronto, 1910, by W. F. Ganong.

FOLKLORE NOTES FROM THE NEWFOUND-LAND BAND

In the ancient Micmac nomenclature of Newfoundland are a few names connected with Beothuk history. Red Indian lake is *Meγwe'djewa''gi'*, "Red Indian lake." The various Red Indian camp-sites, the old deer fences, and especially the large campsite at Red Indian point (pl. XXXIII), are familiar to all the present-day Indians. The melancholy history of their former congeners and speculations as to their ultimate fate are subjects that appeal strongly to the Micmac. In general the idea that the Micmac-Montagnais aided in the remorseless activities against the Beothuk arouses somewhat indignant denial among them. Despite the fact that historical notices, most of which I find have been disseminated from only one or two sources, mention the Micmac among the persecutors of the Red Indians, it must be confessed that I myself am rather skeptical on the point. The Micmac sincerely profess pity for the unfortunate tribe, and commiserate their hard life in the interior, terrified as they fancy by the encroachments of people with firearms, and driven away from the benefit of intercourse with those who could have furnished them with modern utensils and religion. The Indians of Newfoundland today regard the Red Indians as a people who were doomed to their fate through an unconquerable fear of their fellow-men, Micmac as well as Euro-

pean. In a way it might throw light upon
the situation to refer to the fact that the
Montagnais of Labrador, I find, regard their
neighbors, the Naskapi of the interior, in
the same light. It is common to hear Montagnais hunters from the coast relate how,
when they chanced upon a remote camp of
Naskapi in their wanderings, the latter fled
in fear before those who were clothed in
white men's garments.

Returning to the subject of local nomenclature, there is another place known to the
English as Hodge's mountain, some distance northeast of the village of Badger's
Brook. This is called *Meɣweʿzaʹxsit*, "red-
faced person." It is claimed that a Micmac hunter many years ago discovered a
Red Indian camp on its slopes. Everything was intact in a lone wigwam discovered there, which was lined with caribou-
skins (incidentally another Algonkian resemblance). Here, Louis John claims, is
where the last Red Indians are thought to
have starved to death during a severe winter storm.

Some historical accounts from Indian

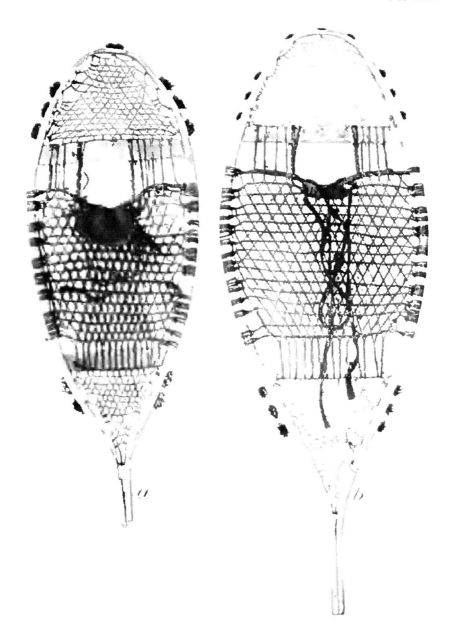

SNOWSHOES OF THE BADGER'S BROOK BAND OF MICMAC

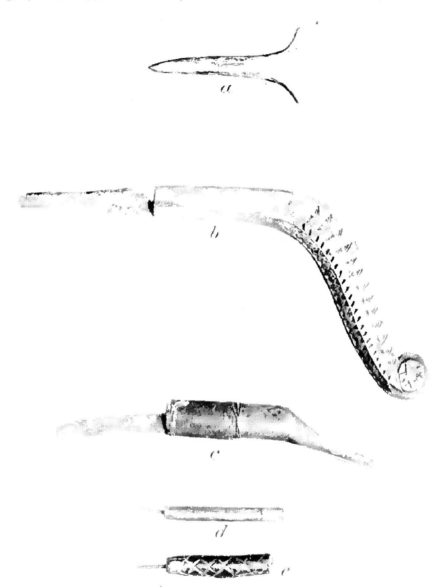

PICK. AWLS AND KNIVES OF THE BADGER'S BROOK BAND OF MICMAC

a, Antler pick for punching meat to be smoke-dried. *b*, *c*, Crooked knives (*waγa'γan*). *d*, Iron awl (*sisi'gan*). *e*, Iron awl with carved handle.   Length of *c*. 9¾ in.

sources and some miscellaneous Beothuk lore gathered incidentally in the interior are next presented.[43]

The Story of Buchan's Expedition [44]

(Related by John Paul, of Badger's Brook, Newfoundland, 68 years of age in 1914, who heard it from his grandfather[45])

"Captain Buchan, with a Micmac and a Mountaineer Indian for guides, went to capture some Red Indians. They ascended Exploits river in the winter and with the help of their guides who knew the country well, discovered a Red-Indian camp at Red Indian point,[46] where the chief lived. The Micmac and Mountaineer guide enabled the party to make friends with the people at the camp. Buchan told the Red Indians that he had presents for them back on Exploits river, and said that he would take two of them back with him to get the stuff. So he left two of his own men at the camp. So they started back to the mouth of Exploits. When they got to Rushy pond, caribou footprints were seen and the two Red Indians were told by signals to give chase. The two then started off, not understanding apparently for what reason they were sent away. By the next night they had not returned, and Buchan told the Micmac and Mountaineer to track them. They started on the track and came back to report that the Red Indians' trail led back toward Red Indian lake. So then the whole party started back and reached the camp at Red Indian point.

It was deserted, but the two white men were found beheaded. Then Buchan gave chase, but his party was unable to follow them because there were footprints in confusion all over the snow on the lake. So Buchan went to several of their abandoned camps and put gunpowder in all the fireplaces so that they would blow up when the Red Indians came back to light the fires at their old camps. Afterward, of course, a lot of the Red Indians were killed by the device.

"Some time later John Peyton and another man (named Day?) went to the interior to capture some Red Indians. They struck the headwaters of Mary March brook and went down walking on the ice until they came to the mouth, at the north arm of Red Indian lake. This is now Mary March's point, right at the village of Millertown.[47] Here they found a family camping. They approached slyly and took the family by surprise. They took hold of the woman, Mary March, and her husband came to her aid. They then shot five balls into him before he fell. He was a very big man, seven feet tall, as they measured him with their feet while he lay at full length on the ice. Mary March then pointed out to the white men her full breasts to show that she had a child, and pointed up to the heavens to implore them, in God's mercy, to allow her to return to her child. But they took her away with them and returned to St John where she died after a while.

"My grandfather [John Paul speaking] remembered when he went to St John and saw

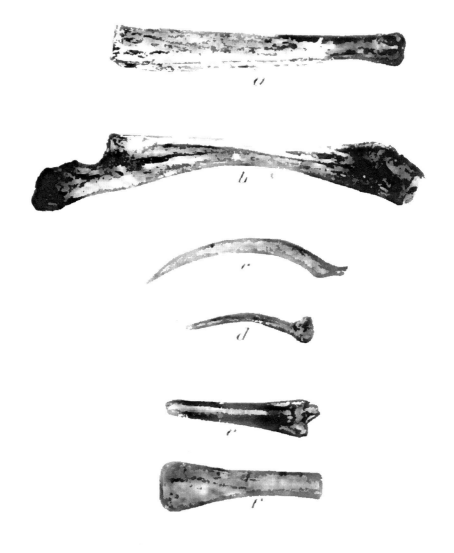

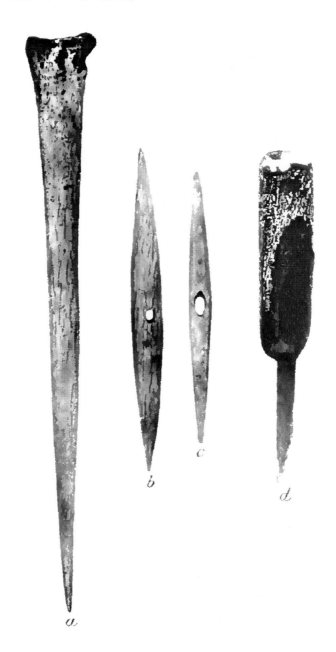

PUNCH, NEEDLES, AND CHISEL OF THE BADGER'S BROOK BAND OF MICMAC

(*a*, caribou-bone punch for regulating mesh of snowshoe filling (*ilewe'gan*); 7½ in. long. *b*, Snowshoe needle of caribou-bone (*laiwi'gan*). *c*, Snowshoe needle of caribou antler. *d*, Iron chisel (*waliski'gan, zabiski'gan*) for cutting mortise holes in snowshoe frames

Mary March. At the time he wore a pair of caribou-skin boots. Poor Mary, when she saw the boots, pointed to them and was so glad to see something that reminded her of her people. My grandfather thought she was very good-looking and of a fair complexion. They used red clay to color themselves with, which is known to abound in certain localities on Exploits river and Red Indian lake."

A Meeting Between a Red Indian's Family and a Micmac Family

(Also by John Paul's dictation)

"My grandfather and grandmother were once coming up Exploits river in their canoe. Suddenly coming around a bend they beheld a Red Indian and his wife in a canoe coming down. When the Red Indian saw them he quickly paddled ashore and he and his wife hurried into the woods to hide, taking only his bow and arrows. The Micmac paddled alongside the empty canoe and there saw a small child lying in the bottom, but there was nothing to eat in the canoe. Then my grandfather said to his wife: 'They have nothing to eat and must be going down to the bay [Exploits bay] for fish. Let us put some of our smoked meat in their canoe.' So he put some meat in for a present and paddled on. When they got around the point, they went ashore and walked back through the thicket to where they could see the Red Indian's canoe. They beheld the Red Indian soon come down to his canoe, look in, then beckon to his wife, who came out. Then he pointed out to her the meat in the canoe. Then he pointed to where my grandfather had gone up-river in his canoe and paddled off."

An Encounter with Red Indians near Twillingate

(Told by an old man at Millertown Junction)

"Near Twillingate the fishermen often went into the interior to hunt and trap, leaving their women folks home until their return. One time an old fellow went hunting, and during his absence one night a couple of Red Indians came and got upon the roof of the shack. The fisherman's wife got frightened and called to her children to bring the gun. As soon as the Red Indians heard the word 'gun,' which they seemed to understand, they fled."

An Encounter near Dildo Arm

(Told by Mr Hartigan at Millertown)

"One time near Dildo Arm some hunters who went into the woods left their guns at their camp, not suspecting any danger. Some Red Indians discovered the camp and were examining the outfit. The young white men hid and watched the Indians. One of the Indians was peeking down the barrel of a gun which was loaded, while another was fingering around the trigger. The gun suddenly went off and blew off the head of the Indian. They were very wild and unsophisticated people, and fled in terror."

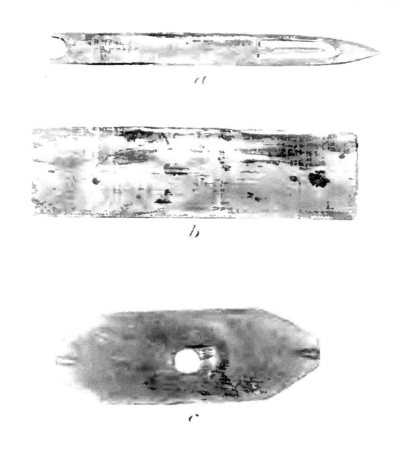

WOODEN NETTING IMPLEMENTS OF THE BADGER'S BROOK

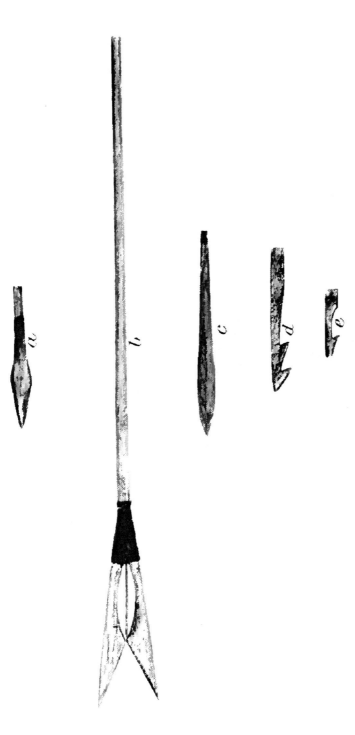

HARPOON-HEADS, LANCE-HEADS, AND FISH-SPEAR OF THE BADGER'S BROOK
BAND OF MICMAC

a, Antler harpoon-head, smooth sides, for killing caribou. *b*, Model of fish-spear (*neγo'γɛl*); *c*, Antler harpoon for killing caribou. *d*, Antler harpoon-head, double barb, for killing seals. *e*, Antler harpoon-head for killing beaver

Miscellaneous Anecdotes

A. (Told by William Beaton, a Micmac-Montagnais at Badger's Brook)

"There was once, it is told, a large schooner loaded with fifty tierces of codfish anchored off the shore in Twillingate bay. The crew had gone ashore, and during one night the schooner was boarded by some Red Indians and dismantled. When the crew returned they found all her sails cleared away and her ropes all gone. All her instruments and clocks were also taken. The Red Indians took everything in the outfit. They used the sails for tents and clothing. Years afterward the works of the clocks stolen from this schooner, it is supposed, were found by some hunters on the shores of Exploits river."

B. (Told by Mr Tuck, of Millertown, who, when he was a boy, heard it from John Day himself)

John Day, who died some years ago at Springdale, was with Peyton when he captured Mary March. They had to kill her husband by shooting seven balls into him. Then he sat down and could not move any more after the seventh shot. Mary March showed the men her breasts full for her sucking child, but nevertheless they carried her away."

C. (Told by Louis John, a Micmac-Montagnais at Badger's Brook)

"Ben Jore's grandfather was killed by the Red Indians near the mouth of Exploits river.

They cut off his head, put it on a pole, and danced around it."

D. (Told by an old Scotchman at Millertown Junction, recalling memories of his youth. He added, "The Red Indians were such bad people I fancy it was no sin to kill them!")

"The last evidence of the Red Indians was seen at Grand lake by a hunter many years ago. One year he saw a big smoke on an island in the lake. A canoe-load of Indians was seen going from the shore to the island. The hunter was afraid to investigate further at the time, but the next year he went to the same place. This time, however, he did not see any more traces of the Indians."

As an instance of the friendly relations claimed by the Micmac-Montagnais with the Red Indians, which I have already mentioned, Louis John, quoted above, says that his grandfather's father was employed by the English to guide them to Red Indian lake to try to capture some Red Indians. When he found a Red Indians' camp he would tell the poor folk to run, and then he would return and tell the Englishmen that he saw some Red Indians, but that they ran off. "The Micmacs never molested the Red Indians," declared Louis John.

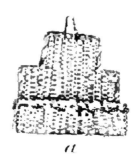

a

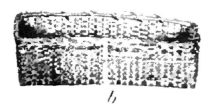

b

c

d

e

SPLINT BASKETRY OF THE BADGER'S BROOK BAND O
MICMAC

a

b

c

BIRCH-BARK BOXES OF THE BADGER'S BROOK BAND OF MICMAC

a, Box covered with porcupine-quill work. *b*, Very old birch-bark and wooden box, covered with quillwork, made by old "Aunt Ellen" Paul, oldest of the Newfoundland Micmac. *c*, Birch-bark box with cover

THE CASE OF SANTU

The most surprising occurrence, however, in recent years concerning the fate of the Beothuk Indians was the accidental dis-covery of an old Indian woman named Santu, who claimed that her father was one of the last survivors of the Red Indians of Newfoundland. Since considerable discus-sion was aroused over the innocent claim of the old woman when I had made it public, I shall give the circumstances in some detail, for the benefit of those who may wish to determine to what extent her testimony may be relied on, before making use of the information and the brief vocabulary obtained from her.

Mr James P. Howley, Director of the Geological Survey of Newfoundland, who for more than forty years has been inter-ested in the history of the Beothuk, during a visit I made him at St Johns in 1914, expressed his unbelief in Santu's veracity.[48] Notwithstanding the fact that Mr Howley's opinions, based on his extensive knowledge of Newfoundland history and physiography, deserve serious consideration, I hardly think, under the curcumstances, that the conclusions of one trained in sciences other than ethnology are sufficient to warrant absolutely casting aside information which may be of value, and which on the face of it does bear some semblance of truthfulness.

In July, 1910, I happened to talk over ethnological matters with a family of Micmac who were temporarily camped near Gloucester, Mass. The family consisted of an aged woman, her son, his wife and child (pl. XXXIV-XXXVI). They all spoke Micmac. The family name was Toney. On inquiring of the young man, Joe Toney, where he was born, he told me in Newfoundland. Then becoming more interested, I inquired if his mother was a native of Newfoundland, and he replied that she was. After a few minutes' talk with his mother, he said that she was not a true Micmac, but that her father was an *Osa'γan'a* Indian from Red Pond, Newfoundland. This naturally startled me, because it referred indirectly to the supposedly extinct Beothuk. Further conversation with the young man, who translated

a

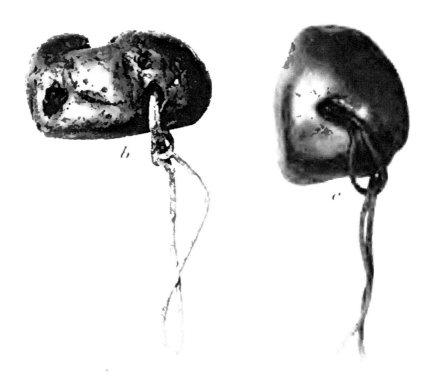

FETISH OBJECTS OF THE BADGER'S BROOK BAND OF MICMA
  a, Hunter's luck-charm of lynx-teeth. *b, c*, Hunter's luck-charr
(*kæundew*) of stone, kept about the house on a string

MICMAC DOLL REPRESENTING "RED INDIAN" (BEOTHUK)

my questions to his mother, disclosed the
fact that she was endeavoring to explain to
me that, while her mother was a Micmac
woman, her father was a member of the
tribe which had been exterminated in the
island by white men. There was at this
time in her statements no idea of boasting,
nor of gaining money or favor. She did not
claim to know any words of her father's
language, but declared her willingness, if I
would give her time, to try to recall some.
On one thing she was definite at the very
first: that her father claimed that he had
been stained red when he was a baby among
his own people, and that his people were
very crude and were persecuted by the
English. He had, it seems, been taken by
the Micmac when he was young, reared by
them, and converted to Christianity. As
for the rest, suffice to say that I spent time
when possible during the rest of the summer
in following the family about from one summer resort to another, encouraging the old
lady, through her son, to endeavor to recall
all that she could of what she had heard her
father narrate of his early life and people,

The old woman was very difficult to work with; because of growing senility she was unable to concentrate her attention on any one thing for a sufficient length of time really to accomplish anything. Petty family troubles and present ills consumed her interest. And so by eking out reminiscences of that period of her life when she lived with her father in Newfoundland, I tediously gathered the information that follows. In September I lost traces of the family, which, I learned later, had moved to Attleboro, Mass.[49] Knowing the old woman's manner and the circumstances, I am convinced that she was not intentionally fabricating a story. My only distrust of the material she was able to give lies in the accuracy of her memory, especially in regard to her vocabulary.

THE INFORMANT'S HISTORY

Santu was born in Newfoundland near "Red Pond" (Red Indian lake), about seventy-five years ago (dating from 1912). Her father, "*Kop*" (name of a red root found in the lake, according to her vocabulary),[50]

VIEW OF THE COUNTRY FORMERLY THE COMMON PROPERTY OF MICMAC AND
BEOTHUK. ACCORDING TO TRADITION

Looking eastward up St George's (formerly Main) river, from near St George's bay

SANTU AND HER SON, JOE TONEY

was a full-blood native of a tribe which called itself *Osa'γan'a*. The name is also known among the Micmac as *Osa'γan'a*. With her father she left Newfoundland at about the age of ten, or a little less, and removed to Nova Scotia, where she passed her early womanhood. Her mother was a Micmac woman, one of the band who lived in Newfoundland. She died, it seems, when Santu was quite young. When Santu grew up, she married a Mohawk and spent part of her time in New Brunswick and Nova Scotia, and part in roaming about in the neighborhood of the Great Lakes with her Mohawk husband until the Civil War broke out, when, to escape being drafted, he led her wandering again throughout the northeastern states and eastern Canada. Her husband then died. Santu returned to Nova Scotia and married a Micmac chief near Yarmouth, whose name was Toney. Living there a while, she had four or five children, and finally, with her youngest son, separated from her husband and since then has been drifting about the New England states with him, earning an uncertain living

by basket-making, bead-working, and for-
tune-telling. Her one son, Joe Toney, still
lives with her. He has married a Micmac
woman of Nova Scotia, and they have one
child (1912).

ETHNOLOGICAL NOTES

Santu remembers in her childhood having
traveled with her father in the skin canoes
which seem to have been one of the types
of craft in use by the *Osa'yan'a*.[51] While
the details of construction given by Santu
were very vague, it seems that the canoe
was more of a kayak. It was about fifteen
feet in length and about two and a half in
width, constructed on a wooden framework
with a caribou- or seal-skin covering sewed
with water-tight seams. The seams were
sewed by laying the two edges together,
bending them over and sewing the three
thicknesses together. Bone awls, she said,
were used to perforate the holes for the
stitches. The bow of the canoe, she re-
marked, was straightened and stiffened by a
piece of spruce-bark (*sic*),[52] and another
curved piece held the stern in shape. The

JOE TONEY

bottom was found. At the back sat the man with his paddle. The whole front of the craft was covered with the skin, forming an enclosure large enough to contain the whole family, including women, children, dogs, and property. At his side and in front of him the man had his harpoon and other necessaries fastened on the side of the deck. It is to be understood from this description that a covered kayak-like type of boat is described. The skin-covering of the canoe was so arranged that it could be wrapped around the waist of the man so that no water could come into the hold in rough weather. In this craft the family traveled all over the country by waterways and coast. day and night. When a landing and camp were to be made the cover would be taken off the canoe, poles cut for a wigwam, and a temporary camp made until it was time to move on. Santu herself remembers being bundled in with dogs and members of her family, and traveling by night and day with her father.

The people, she claimed, subsisted largely on sea mammals' flesh and caribou, using the harpoon for killing the former and the bow and arrow for the latter. When an animal was killed with an arrow, the arrow was never used again, but thrown away as a kind of sacrifice.

Flesh to be eaten was thrown on the fire and only partly roasted. Her father, she remembers, would eat little or no vegetal food nor bread. His diet consisted mostly of half-roasted meat.

A certain species of leaves was smoked in stone pipes.[53]

Allowance should be made for the probability that in some of these descriptions the old woman's memory was so hazy that she could not distinguish between what she intended to claim as applying to the customs of her father's people and those of the Micmac-Montagnais among whom they lived.

The most interesting information is that describing an annual ceremony participated in by the tribe at "Red Pond." It took place in the spring of the year when the tribe gathered and enjoyed, to use Santu's phrase, "a big time." Games were played, among them the dice-and-bowl game in two forms. One of these was with seven dice discs and a bowl,[54] and seventeen counters—four square ones and a crooked one called the "chief." The other form of the game was played with one large die, about two inches across, and six small ones, which were thrown upon a blanket or a hide and struck sidewise with the hand.[55] Men only played the latter. The Micmac and other eastern tribes, she claimed, learned this game originally from her people. It is worthy of note that this game does not occur among the Wabanaki west of the Micmac. Dancing and feasting accompanied the event. At a certain time the men procured quantities of a kind of red root from the lake and squeezed from it the juice which was used for staining their bodies red. The ceremony is said to have lasted about ten days. Every person in the tribe was dyed. Children who were born during the year away in the hunting territories were brought to this ceremony for the first time and received their coat of dye, which was to last them for the year. It is supposed that under certain conditions the dye could be renewed, though the application of the coloring was regarded as a kind of initiation and mark of tribal identity. One good application is said to have lasted six months. Santu's father, she claimed, was the last child to have been treated in this way. When he grew up he was converted to Catholicism and gave up his belief in the necessity of the red dye. If anyone was observed by the chief to have some of the coloring washed from any part of his body, he was ordered to go to water and wash off his dye as a punishment, and not to renew it until the next ceremony. [56]

Santu heard the tradition from her father that in his grandfather's time (?) a ship was wrecked off the coast of Newfoundland and all hands were drowned except two women who, with the help of the natives, were brought ashore. One of them shortly afterward died; the other remained with the tribe, married one of the men, and spent her life there. Her father thought that he was descended from this woman.

Several opinions expressed by Santu regarding her father's people may be of value.

One was in reply to a direct question as to whether her father's people were of mixed Eskimo and Indian blood. Friendly relations, she said, were maintained with the Labrador Eskimo and Indians. Some of her father's people, she said, when dispersed, joined them. She remembers, while living in Nova Scotia, a paternal uncle or great-uncle returning from Greenland where he had emigrated and intermarried with the Eskimo there. He claimed that others of their people were in Greenland, all intermarried with Eskimo, and that there were a number of children. He died there within six months after coming to Nova Scotia. Santu stated that she had a relative (I fail to recall whether it was a cousin or a brother) somewhere who knew a great deal of the *Osa'γan'a* language.

The Micmac, she said, came to Newfoundland a long time ago and for a while, with the white people, fought her people. Afterward a number intermarried with the *Osa'γan'a*, some of the descendants of the latter being still scattered here and there among the Micmac of Newfoundland and elsewhere.

There seems little doubt from Santu's statements that *Osa'γɑnʹa* descendants may be found in the maritime provinces and that the tribal name itself is one of the native terms for the tribe known in history as the Beothuk.

Santu, with great difficulty during the summer, remembered the following words in her father's language:

be'nɑm, woman (Micmac and Malecite *épit*, Penobscot *pʻhe'nɑm*).
gu'wa, fat person (Micmac *me'gigit*).
gau, rain (Micmac *giˑkpesaʻʹ*).
hɑᵍ, baby cradle, or cradle-board.
tuˑᵇ, baby blanket (Micmac *wobiʹʹsun*).
se'ko, prayer (Micmac *alasuʹʹdma*).
siˑkane'sˑu, whale (Micmac *po'dɑp*, Penobscot -*esˑu,* "living creature," noun ending in animal names).
NOTE: ᵍ, ᵇ, weakly articulated final consonants.

Her father's people, Santu alleged, used their hands a great deal in conversation. The only word in the above list in which any resemblance can be recognized as occurring in any of the published Beothuk lists is the term *be'nam*, "woman." Compare *emam-* (*emamoose*), "woman" (Peyton vocabulary; (Lloyd in *Journal of the Anthropological Institute of Great Britain and Ireland*, 1875), and *enam*, "woman," given by Patterson in *Transactions of the Royal Society of Canada*, vol. x.

Among other reminiscences I add the following song, transcribed by Mr J. D. Sapir from a phonograph record made by Santu while she was camped at Hampton Beach, N. H., in 1910. It was a rendition of a song that she had learned from her father when she was a girl. She claimed that her father told her that it was an *Osa'γan'a* song.

The syllables were too inarticulate to be taken down at the time, I am sorry to say. Santu stated that she was unable to explain them, because they had no sequence of meaning to her.

Again during my trip in Newfoundland I inquired of several elderly Indians about the woman Santu. John Paul, already mentioned, knew of a woman of Santu's description who had gone to Nova Scotia

SANTU'S SONG.

68

and was there the wife of a wealthy Micmac chief named Toney. He furthermore, much to my inward surprise, credited the claim that her father had been a man of Red Indian blood. He stated that the thing was not only possible, but that it might well be expected to be true, considering the sedentary habits of many of the Micmac hunters and the secretiveness of the Indians concerning the Red Indians a generation or so ago through fear of retaliation or at least molestation at the hands of the English, since such a stir had been raised over them. From Micmac in Newfoundland I even learned of another man, George McCloud, whom no one could locate at the time. He was said to have knowledge not only of the Red Indian language, but also of where descendants could still be found in Labrador.

If, despite the meagerness of our actual knowledge of the tribe, any conclusions are at all permissible, I believe the indications will increasingly show that the Beothuk formed an archaic member of the culture group which embraced the Micmac and the other northeastern Algonkian. This is a strong corroboration of the evidence of linguistic relationship with the Algonkian. As for the likelihood of Eskimo relationship, the links of union, either archeological or otherwise, are not a bit stronger than between the Eskimo and the Montagnais. The next thing to be done in this field, aside from systematic archeological research, is to collect a sufficient quantity of mythological material from the Newfoundland Indians for comparison with that of the Micmac of the mainland in order to determine, if possible, traces of what might be considered Beothuk influence.

NOTES

1. The primary object of the expedition, if it might be called one, was to trace the remains among the Micmac of the old Algonkian institution of the family hunting territory, which was first mentioned in this region by Le Clercq in 1691. The results form part II of this paper.

2. C. C. Willoughby, Prehistoric Burial Places in Maine, *Archaeological and Ethnological Papers of the Peabody Museum*, vol. 1, no. 6, Cambridge, 1898.

3. W. K. Moorehead, The Red Paint People of Maine, *American Anthropologist*, vol. 15, no. 1, 1913.

4. F. G. Speck, An Ancient Archeological Site on the Lower St Lawrence, *Holmes Anniversary Volume*, Washington, 1916.

5. J. P. Howley, The Beothuks or Red Indians of Newfoundland . . ., Cambridge University Press. 1915.

6. Mr Howley (op. cit., p. xix) in his introduction rather indefinitely favors the theory of Athabascan affinity. He says: "On the authority of the late Sir William Dawson . . . a tradition existed among the Micmac tribes of Nova Scotia that a previous people occupied that territory whom the Micmacs drove out and who were probably allied to the Tinné or Chippewan stock. These, he thinks, may have passed over to Newfoundland and become the progenitors of the Beothuks. This supposition appears to me to carry with it a considerable amount of proba-

bility. Here, isolated and undisturbed for several centuries, untainted by inter-mixture with other tribes, they could retain all their original traits of character, language, etc., which remained with them as distinctive features down to the last moments of their existence. . . . . Under all circumstances surrounding this mysterious tribe, we must only fall back upon the suggestion of Sir William Dawson as the most plausible theory to account for their presence here."

7. The derivation of this term is not clear to the informants, beyond the plural adjectival suffix—*wi·ak*. In the Micmac names here given, the character γ denotes a velar voiced sperant, *x* the corresponding surd.

8. Page 5) of this paper.

9. W. H. Mechling, Malecite Tales, *Anthropological Series, Geological Survey of Canada*, no. 4, 1914, p. 65.

10. Ibid., p. 65, footnote.

11. Howley, op. cit., p. 286.

12. See also S. T. Rand, Dictionary of the Language of the Micmac Indians, 1888, p. 215. Howley (op. cit., pp. 284–6) gives a Micmac tradition from Nova Scotia relating to the Beothuk. C. G. Leland (Algonquin Legends of New England, Boston, 1885, pp. 206–7), in commenting on a Passamaquoddy tale in which the wolverene marries a red woman whose color rubbed off when she was touched, entertains the rather far-fetched idea

that the tale referred to the "Newfoundland Indians covered with red ochre."

13. Cf. Howley, op. cit., p. 30, where he quotes
Cartwright's description.

14. These fences are known also to the Montagnais of Labrador, who call them
nkɔwagana'ck^w, and were used by the New
England Indians. Cf. The History of
Philip's War, . . . by Thomas Church, Esq.
. . . with an appendix, . . . Samuel G.
Drake, 2nd ed., Exeter, N. H., 1829, p. 340.

15. Anecdotes will later be given. Howley (op.
cit., pp. 91–2, 269, 271, 280) refers to
this activity on the part of the Beothuk.

16. Résumé of material quoted from part II of
this volume.

17. The same omen is found generally throughout the tribes of the Wabanaki group.

18. Rand, op. cit., p. 200. An almost identical
tale among the Passamaquoddy accounts
for the hostility between them and the Mohawk. (Cf. J. D. Prince, Passamaquoddy
Documents, *Annals of N. Y. Academy
of Science*, 1898, vol. XI, no. 15, p. 371.)

19. Several historical sources agree on this
point, Cormack, Howley, and Jukes.
Howley (op. cit., pp. 25–26) quotes a tradition from J. B. Jukes, Excursions in
Newfoundland, London, 1842, p. 129.

20. Cf. Howley, op. cit., pp. 29–30, quoting
Cartwright's Journal. Cartwright describes the construction of the square or
winter camp of logs placed horizontally
to form the lower part, and the bark
pyramidal roof. The hoop, he says,

appear near the top of the roof. The hoop seems to be a feature differentiating the wigwam construction of the tribes of the Waban·ki and M ntag ais groups from that of all other northern peoples of America. Consult also Howley (op. cit., p. 245 and sketch VI), who mentions this feature of construction.

21. Cf. W. C. Orchard, Notes on Penobscot Houses, *American Anthropologist*, vol. II, no. 4 (1909), p. 602.

22. Howley, op. cit., pp. 31–33, quotes Cartwright in full and also gives figures of miniature canoes in his own collection (pls. XXXI, XXXIV).

23. Cormack in his Journal says that the Micmac whom he met in the interior of the island told him that the Red Indians used skin canoes similar to their own (quoted by Howley, op. cit., p. 152, also p. 213)

24. This information is confirmed by Denys (1672), who describes in some detail the method of applying the colors. (Cf. Nicholas Denys, The Description and Natural History of the Coasts of North America, edition of the Champlain Society, Toronto, 1908, by W. F. Ganong, p. 411.) Le Clercq mentions the same thing. (Cf. Chrestien Le Clercq, New Relation of Gaspesia, edition of the Champlain Society, Toronto, 1910. by W. F. Ganong, p. 96.)

25. Another name is *te'bu't'k'*, a term possibly of English origin, from "the boots." Cf. also Rand, Micmac Dictionary, p. 41.

26. Footwear made of the leg skin or hock of the caribou is mentioned as a characteristic of the Beothuk (Howley, op. cit., pp. 271, 322). The same thing is common among the Micmac and the rest of the northern and eastern Algonkian.

27. Rand (Micmac Dictionary, p. 161) has *ŭltâktă'gŭnă'*, "loom," and (p. 278) *ĕltâktăăgă*, "to weave."

28. Mention of weaving on a frame was made by Nicholas Denys (1672). op. cit. Rand (Micmac-English Dictionary, p. 255) gives *wiskobooksoon*, "straps."

29. Rand (Micmac Dictionary, p. 249) gives *mimŭndă'*, "to spin flax on a little wheel."

30. F. G. Speck, The Double Curve Motive in Northeastern Algonkian Art, *Geological Survey of Canada, Anthropological Series*, no. 1, 1914, p. 11, fig. 14.

31. Rand (Micmac Dictionary, p. 201) gives *moolsăwă'*, "pouch."

32. Howley (op. cit., p. 87) reproduces Cartwright's figure of a Beothuk snowshoe in which the shape and proportions are almost identical with those of the ordinary Micmac article used on the island today (see pl. XXIII). The dimensions of the Beothuk shoe are given as: width 15 inches, body 3½ feet, tail 1 foot, which are about the same as those of the specimens just referred to.

33. For these terms Rand (op. cit., p. 151) gives *wâkagŭn'igŭn*, "crooked knife," (p. 178)

tādooĭgŭn, "snowshoe needle," and *sakŭde,* "needle."

34. For these implements Rand (Micmac Dictionary, p. 129) has: *ŭpskaoo,* "harpoon," *sĕmoogwŏde,* "spear," and *negok,* "salmon spear" (p. 246).

35. Supposedly a corruption of French *panier.* Rand (Micmac Dictionary, p. 31), *peotă-leāuā.*

36. I have introduced a brief treatment of the northward spread of splint basketry in Decorative Art and Basketry of the Cherokee, *Bulletin of the Public Museum of Milwaukee,* vol. 2, no. 2, 1920.

37. Bark vessels and baskets were common Beothuk manufactures (Howley, op. cit., pp. 249, 214 and sketch VII, and pl. XXXI, XXXIV). The types and details of stitching are the same as in the ordinary Indian specimens. In the Beothuk names for these receptacles, *guinya butt,* "water bucket" (also *booch-moot,* "seal stomach oil bag"), we recognize cognate Algonkian —*mint'* (Montagnais), *-ut'* (Malecite), and *-udi* (Penobscot), "receptacle."

38. Howley, op. cit., p. 340 and pl. XXV.

39. Quoting John Paul.

40. Article on Beothuk in Handbook of American Indians, *Bulletin 30, Bureau of American Ethnology,* part I, p. 142.

41. This negative information cannot be relied on, as several accounts contradict one another on the point. Cf. Howley (pp. 19–20), quoting Richard Whitbourne, A Discourse a d Discovery of the Newe-

founde-launde, London 1622, and also Howley, p. 221.

42. Bonnycastle, R. H., Newfoundland in 1842 (London, 1842). Whatever may be the tree referred to by this unique name, it could hardly be the pine of the region, Bank's or jack pine. All northern Indians know that inner birch rind and even poplar can be made to yield a little nourishment in times of famine, but seldom pine bark.

43. Howley (op. cit., pp. 265–288) records a number of anecdotes, some of which might be considered as variants of those given here.

44. In 1801 Lieutenant Buchan, of the Royal Navy, was sent to the River Exploits to winter there and to open communication with the Indians. He succeeded in finding a party of them. Inducing two of their number to go with him as hostages, and leaving two marines with the Indians at the main camp as a pledge of good faith, he returned to his depot for presents. During his absence the fears of the Red Indians were aroused, lest from his delay in returning he might bring up reinforcements with a view of capturing them. In the meantime one of the two Red Indians took fright and fled back to the main camp. They murdered the hostages and fled to the interior. This was at Red Indian lake, near the mouth of Mary March brook. In 1819 a female was taken by a party of trappers on Red In-

dian lake. Her husband was with her, and having offered resistance was shot. The leader of the men of the party was named Peyton. The woman was brought to St John's and was named Mary March, from the month in which she was taken. She was treated with kindness and sent back to her friends with numerous presents, but died on the voyage, having been suffering for some time with consumption. Her body was placed in a coffin and left on the margin of the lake, so that it might be found by her relatives. The latter conveyed it to their burying place on Red Indian lake, where it was found several years later by Cormack, lying beside the body of her murdered husband.

45. John Paul had been a headman among the Micmac-Montagnais of the island and was particularly well-informed in matters of native life. His age, experience, and willingness to help in this work made him invaluable, and I take this occasion to recommend him to others who may undertake similar studies in this region where the younger generation of natives is not well informed nor conservative.

46. This is Red Indian point, on Red Indian lake; see pl. I–V. A larger excavation than the others at this site is pointed out as the chief's wigwam.

47. The lumbermen who have recently invaded this region have fortunately spared a large spruce tree which is popularly believed

to be the tree under which Mary March was captured. It stands on a sandy point called Mary March's point, and archeological evidences here indicate a former camp. This tree, which is now (1914) in danger of falling, is shown in pl. v.

48. Previously to this Mr Howley had indicated in a letter that he thought the informant was making her claim for the purpose of gain.

49. Later, in the following spring, Mr R. S. Dahl, a former associate of Mr Howley, who was also deeply interested in the Beothuk, came to Philadelphia to see me concerning Santu. When, however, he went to Attleboro to trace them, the family had left. Since then Joe Toney has returned irregularly to Gloucester, Mass., where I have seen him. His mother in 1916 had returned to Yarmouth, Nova Scotia, where her husband died recently. (Since this was written I have heard that she died in 1919.)

50. Incidentally, Cope is a common family surname among the Nova Scotia Micmac, see page 103. I do not regard this information as strictly reliable.

51. We recognize in this the common craft of the Newfoundland Micmac.

52. She evidently referred to the curved keelson of spruce forming the ends.

53. Compare Howley (op. cit., p. 322) for reference to stone pipes.

54. The common Micmac and Wabanaki game of *wallesta'yan.*

55. This corresponds with the Micmac game of
    wabəna'ɣan, played with eight ivory discs,
    or dice, an inch in diameter. The play-
    ers, who may be of any number, take
    turns throwing the discs upon a blanket.
    There are only three throws that count.
    A throw showing two discs with the same
    side up counts one (*ma'xtewi' txamo'wi*);
    one only facing up and seven opposite,
    count five (*wa'bitewi' txamo'wi*). Should
    a player throw all, flat side down the same
    way, it is called *mi'ktcik tciwa'wal*,
    "turtle eggs," and wins the game. The
    above is the manner in which it is
    played in Cape Breton.
56. Cormack records that the Beothuk never
    washed "except when a husband or a wife
    died" (Howley, p. 230).

BEOTHUK AND MICMAC

PART II

MICMAC HUNTING TERRITORIES IN NOVA SCOTIA AND NEWFOUNDLAND

BY

FRANK G. SPECK

II. MICMAC HUNTING TERRI-TORIES IN NOVA SCOTIA AND NEWFOUNDLAND

By Frank G. Speck

INTRODUCTION

THE subject of the family hunting territory which provides the keynote to the social organization of the northern and eastern Algonkian tribes has become by this time fairly familiar to ethnologists, first through the reports of surveys which I have so far completed for the Division of Anthropology of the Geological Survey of Canada (by whose sanction this paper is published), and later through the handling of the situation as a sociological phenomenon by Dr. R. H. Lowie in his recent treatise.[1] No one would now deny that here is to be found one of the most fundamental properties of old Algonkian culture; that here is an exceedingly primitive group showing the developed idea of established geographical claims. And of still more importance, it has become apparent that in this relatively primitive level, patrilineality occurs as a social feature chronologically anterior to the matrilineal grouping, and even culturally below it. The general applicability of theories of social evolution, like those of Bachofen, Morgan, and Hartland, which insist on the priority of the matrilineal grouping, are destined to assume a more and more dubious aspect as intensive exploration proceeds into the social life of hitherto little-known and loosely organized tribes. It remains, therefore, as a most urgent task to prosecute the survey of the primitive nomadic tribes of the Hudsonian and Arctic zones for the full census of those whose social organization is based on the paternal family and who observe the family hunting territorial divisions. When this has been done, speculations may be expected to take a more final form. There are still large areas to traverse and to map out, and there are varied types of social structure to be analyzed, in which minor developments have appeared and become associated with the territorial units. In the accompanying report, the hunting group is traced in the maritime provinces eastward to the Atlantic, thus covering one more large area in the gradual spread of our knowledge. Surveys are already partially completed for the region lying from Lake Waswanipi in northern Quebec southward to the St Lawrence and eastward to Portneuf river.

In some parts of this zone there are specific variations. Among the Ojibwa, for instance, a strong feature is the interassociation of the biological family group with the patrilineal exogamic gens. Among the Montagnais the absence of the gens is noteworthy, but the development of the geographical feature stands forth in the district names. At Penobscot there is the association of family ancestry with animals, approaching the idea of the so-called "use totem," discussed by Rivers and Goldenweiser. Our present case shows the Mic-

mac to present little to mark their form of
the institution with distinctive emphasis.
Here the family territories seem to be less
permanent, less hereditary, than elsewhere,
and the judicial power of the chief in the
reassignment of territory seems to be rather
more definite.   In other respects a comparison of the Micmac hunting territory institution with that of neighboring tribes seems
to show an absence of specialization in the
case of the former.

HUNTING TERRITORIES IN NOVA SCOTIA

The Micmac, like the rest of the northern
and eastern Algonkian, whose subsistence
was gained by hunting and fishing, had
their country subdivided into more or less
well recognized districts in which certain
individual proprietors or families enjoyed
the inherited privilege of hunting.   Having
already made this matter the subject of in-
vestigations during several seasons among
the   Montagnais,   Mistassini,   northern
Ojibwa, Algonquin, and the Penobscot and
Abnaki of the east. I spent part of the
summer of 1914 in visiting the settlements

of the Micmac of Nova Scotia, Cape Breton, and Newfoundland, to make collateral
studies among the most easterly branches of
the Algonkian stock. The social organization of this people is also characterized
by a grouping into hunting families, and
it also shows the second associated feature;
it is extremely loose in general. The results
of my survey are presented in this paper.

It should be remembered by anyone taking up this subject of family groupings and
territorial claims from the sociological
point of view, that, in contrast with the
north central Algonkians (Ojibwa, Algonquin), there is no intercrossing among the
Micmac of a clan organization with the
family group. Neither exogamy nor other
elements of group totemism are now found
here as among the Ojibwa, Algonquin,
or even the Penobscot, who have indeed
some semblance of the animal totemic group
formation manifested in such phenomena as
family explanation myths, group naming,
emblems, and a certain social identity within
the group. It is true of the Micmac
throughout, so far as I could learn, that the

family groups and their hunting territories, whether held by the group in common or by individuals, are found to rest on a purely economic basis, with no sociological phenomenon other than kinship involved.[2]

We are fortunate in having several notices of the existence of the hunting territory in Father Le Clercq's time (1691), which not only authenticate the matter among the Micmac but which give a fair summary of characteristics. It is necessary that Le Clercq be quoted.

"It is the right of the head of the nation according to the customs of the country, which serve as laws and regulations to the Gaspesians, to distribute the places of hunting (*les endroits de la chasse*) to each individual. It is not permitted to any Indian to overstep the bounds and limits of the region (*d'outre-passer les bornes et les limites du quartier*) which shall have been assigned to him in the assembly of the elders. These are held in autumn and in spring expressly to make this assignment."[3]

Le Clercq also speaks of the territories in another place, using the expression, "The occupation of this chief was to assign the places for hunting (*de regler les lieux de chasse*)."[4] It is important to note that, among the Indians who use Canadian French today, the designations *"lieux de chasse"* and *"endroits de la chasse"* are the same.

Again the same author tells us:

"The most important places for fishing and hunting are marked by the crosses which they set up in the vicinity, and one is agreeably surprised in voyaging through this country to find from time to time upon the borders of the rivers crosses with double and triple cross-pieces like those of the patriarchs."[5]

Any question as to the antiquity or the nativity of the institution we are interested in among the Micmac is decisively met by these statements. Nicholas Denys, who wrote about Micmac customs nineteen years earlier than Le Clercq, does not, however, refer specifically to it, although he speaks briefly of the conservation of the game which is often an accompanying feature.

"They killed the animals only in proportion as they had need of them. When they were tired of eating one sort, they killed some of another."[6]

The Micmac family group seems to have possessed a rather unstable character. It consisted of the father of the family, his wife and children, and other members of his own kin who, through individual circumstances, might be left to his support. Generally the family included the living grandparents, and frequently aunts, uncles, and even relatives by marriage. Accordingly, the content of the group changed as the children became married and left, or increased as bereaved relatives were added. It was a common practice for a man to join his father-in-law's family for a time after marriage among the Micmac as well as among the other northern tribes covered so far by the investigation. The Micmac newly-married man generally did this unless local conditions made another course advisable. After a year or so with his father-in-law, he was expected to set up a new domestic establishment on hunting grounds acquired through reapportionment or inheritance, or else to settle, should circumstances be favorable, on part of the patrimonial territory under his own identity or that of his father. The family unit was, in respect to its membership, judging from all sources, an exceedingly variable quantity.

A side-light is thrown upon another social aspect of the early Micmac by Le Clercq which shows that here, as elsewhere in the wide area where the family band with its hunting territory takes the place of the clan or gentile unit, numerical strength of the family counts for something in determining social position. Le Clercq says, in speaking of chiefs or leaders:

"We had among us at the River of St Joseph [the Restigouche] one of these old chiefs whom our Gaspesians considered as their head and their ruler, much more because of his family which was very numerous, than because of his sovereign power." [7]

This material puts a very simplified aspect on the family institution here, in contrast with the greater complexity prevailing among the Algonkian farther west. It is difficult to form an opinion yet as to whether the simplicity is a sign of archaism or of degenerated culture in comparison with the other Algonkian. Since I hope to pursue the investigation of this institution through the whole habitat of the northern hunting tribes, if the opportunity offers, we may leave the discussion of the question until more is known of the facts, and proceed directly to the material as it presents itself among the Micmac.

In Nova Scotia I procured data covering nearly the whole peninsula. The portion not covered is the extreme southwestern part of the peninsula, the habitat of the Yarmouth band, which I did not visit. The hunting territory is known here as *tugǝl'wɔ'mi*, derived from a verb meaning "to hunt." The districts generally surround lakes or rivers. They were transmitted from father to son, but where there were no sons to inherit a region it was allotted to someone else. Ordinarily the assignment of hunting districts was left to the authority of the band chief.[8]

The hunters of a certain region had a common rendezvous, generally near the coast where, on occasion, generally in the summer, they assembled with their families for social intercourse. At such times marriages were arranged, and meetings held which resulted in solidifying the group into something of a band. These bands and their gathering places at the present time have grown into the local groups which are found all through the province on small reservations. It may be added that Bear River seems to have been a kind of capital village for the bands in the southwestern part of the province, and Shubenacadie another for the central part. The bands, comprising the localized family groups (see Map I), collectively form the Micmac tribe or nation, the capital village of which is now, as it has been for a very long time, at Eskasoni on Cape Breton island.[9]

The family hunting districts of Nova Scotia with their proprietors' names appear in the accompanying table, the numbers in the first column corresponding with those on the map. I may say that I could not very well verify a large percentage of the districts, since this would have required a personal visit to each family head in the province. However, this was done where it was possible. Hence, being limited largely to material collected from certain informants, chief among whom were

John Brooks and John McEwan of Bear
River, and Jacob Brooks of Truro, I have
probably committed some errors, even
though the individuals relied on were well-
informed leaders. Moreover, the settlement of the province by the English has
encroached on many of the old hunting districts, and some of the proprietors have been
dead so long that it is a matter of question
as to their boundaries even among the oldest men living. Another fact to be observed
is that the boundaries of the family tract
in general among the Micmac were not
so strictly recognized as elsewhere; nor
were they marked by boundary signs, as
among the Penobscot. It seems to suffice
if the main body of water or the general
center of the hunting districts is known, the
line of separation between neighbors being
a general line somewhere about half-way
between the main central landmarks. Retaliation against trespassing was not regu-
larly enforced among the Micmac.

The Micmac country, according to Anderson,[10] was divided into seven districts,
"each having its own chief, but the chief

of the Cape Breton district was looked upon as head of the whole. From Cape Breton three districts stretched to the right, Pictou, Memramcook, Restigouche, and three to the left, Eskegawaage, from Canso to Halifax; Sigunikt, or Shubenacadie, named from Cape Chignecto; and Kaspoogwit, or Annapolis, named from Cape Negro."

This author gives Rand's interpretation of these names in various parts of his report, as follows. *Pictou*, "an explosion, crepitus ventris" (p. 69); *Memramcook*, "variegated landscape" (p. 14); *Restigouche*, "a dead tree" (p. 41). This name has been explained in a number of ways by different authors. One very interesting tale of explanation has been recently published by Father Pacifique in the *Micmac Messenger*, but, unfortunately for ethnology, it is given only in Micmac. *Eskegawaage* is "the skin-dressing place" (p. 27); *Sigunikt*, "a foot cloth, moccasin rag" (p. 22); and *Kaspoogwit*, "land's end," referring to Cape Sable and Cape Negro (p. 35).

Indications appear from time to time in the older writings concerning the tribes of this part of the country to show that animals were frequently employed as symbolic emblems representing different bodies of population. It is difficult, when we encounter such references, to decide whether they are to be understood, from a critical point of view, as the emblems of former gentile or of family groups, or whether they pertain to bands and tribes in the social or linguistic sense. Father LeClercq made note of the observation that the Indians at Miramichi had the figure of a cross as their emblem, while at Restigouche the salmon figured in the same way. He said that each band had its local symbol.[11] Dr Ganong, who edited LeClercq's work, adds that he learned further that the main southwestern division of the Micmac had a sturgeon, the little southwestern division had a beaver, and the northwestern division of the tribe had the figure of a man with a drawn bow and arrow as distinguishing emblems.[12]

For example again, we find in the pictography of the Wabanaki, according to Mallery, who evidently secured the information himself, that the Passamaquoddy are represented by the figure of two men in a canoe following a pollock, both men using paddles;[13] the Malecite by the two men in a canoe both using poles and following a muskrat;[14] the Micmac by the canoemen, both with paddles, following a deer; and the Penobscot by a figure showing the canoemen using pole and paddle following an otter. In giving this information Mallery adds that he thinks the several animals constitute ancient totemic emblems.[15] Incidentally, this affords us another instance of the "game totem" idea which is quite distinctive of the northeastern region, if not particularly true of the Micmac. It is not by any means clear, drawing our ideas from this and other cases which have been recorded among the eastern tribes, how we are to proceed in classifying them as being the totemic concepts of major or of minor social groups. Whether we are to regard them as family or as tribal emblems, the general fact of the game-totem, or use-totem, concept remains established as a feature having a place in the social life of at least some of the members of the group of tribes to which the Micmac belong.[16]

The Micmac have been reported by travelers a number of times as being very capable map-makers, utilizing birch-bark for the purpose of charting not only travel routes but hunting territories as well. Concrete instance of this is afforded by information furnished by Miss Massey of Philadelphia, who states that in 1885 she knew of a case at Digby, Nova Scotia, where a chief who was then about sixty years of age exhibited a birch-bark map of his hunting territory during a trial in court to prove his inherited claim to the same.[17] A map of birch-bark of the land of the Micmac is mentioned as having been given to a hero in one of the legends recorded by Rand.[18] Le Clercq was the earliest author, so far as is known, to have made explicit mention of these charts among the Micmac. He says:

"They have much ingenuity in drawing upon bark a kind of map which marks exactly all the rivers and streams of a country of which they wish to make representation. They mark all the places thereon exactly and so well that they make use of them successfully, and an Indian who possesses one makes long voyages without going astray."[19]

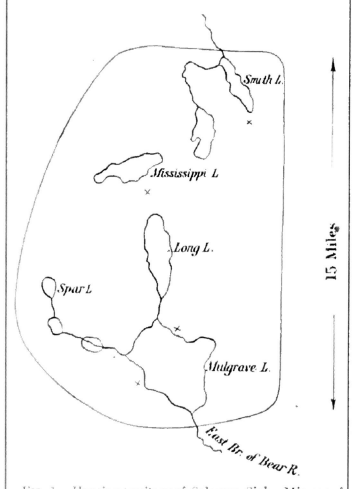

FIG. 3.—Hunting territory of Solomon Siah, Micmac of Bear river, Nova Scotia. (After a drawing by his grandson.)

MICMAC HUNTING ALLOTMENTS IN NOVA SCOTIA

NUMBER ON MAP	NAME OF PROPRIETOR	DISTRICT
	BEAR RIVER BAND	
1	Jim Meuse (*Sa͞´ɣem*, "chief" of this band).	West branch of Bear river to Lake Jolly.
2	John Siah (*Si͞´ya*).	Mulgrave lake neighborhood (see fig. 3).
3	Ben Pictou.	Around Sporting lake, southwest of Bear river.
4	Abram Labrador.	Moosehead and Pine lakes.
5	Joe Penhall.	Pine lake and Cofang lake.
6	John Barriyo.	Long Tusket and Fourth lakes.
7	Christopher Charles.	Barriyo and Spruce lakes.
8	John Louis.	Shelbourne lakes.
9	Joe Maltai and father Old Joe Maltai.	East side of Rossignol lake. West side of Rossignol lake.

10	Louis Luxey (*La′ksi*).	Ponhook lake (divided among his sons).
11	Peter Glode.	Fairy lake and Edjemekudji lake.
12	Frank Charles (*Tcayuli′git*, "short squatty person").	South of Edjemekudji lake.
13	Jack Glode (father of Peter Glode, No. 11).	Upper end of Liverpool lakes.
14	Jim Glode (son of No. 13).	Lower Liverpool lakes almost to Maitland.
15	Stephen Bartlett (*Wisa′u*, "yellow").	Medway lake and part of river.
16	Jim Meuse.	Fifth lake and part of Weymouth river.
	(Joe Salome)	(White Sand lake, but the location cannot well be given.)

Number on Map	Name of Proprietor	District
	ANNAPOLIS BAND	
17	Stephen Hood.	Paradise lakes.
18	— Pictou.	Dalhousie lake and headwaters of Dalhousie river.
19	Louis Labrador.	Upper La Have river.
20	Abe Hood.	Mill creek and Sand river.
21	Ellick Morris.	Gaspereau lakes.
	WINDSOR BAND	
22	Frank Penhall.	Lakes south of Windsor.
23	Tom Phillips.	Ponhook and Caribou lakes.
24	John Hammond.	Lakes near Chester.
25	Joe Brooks.	Uniack lake below Mt Uniack.
26	John Ferris	Kenneticook river valley.

SHUBENACADIE AND SHEET HARBOR BANDS

27	Frank Paul.	Stewiacke river valley.
28	John Newell Cope.	Musquodoboit river between Middle Musquodoboit and Musquodoboit.
29	Andrew Francis.	North of Ship Harbor lake, Gould lake
30	Joe Cope.	North of Jeddore.
31	Young Joe Cope (son of No. 30).	Northeast of Jeddore.
32	Andrew Paul	Grassy lake north of Killag river.
33	(Territory supposed to have belonged to Pauls.)	
34	Sandy Cope.	Tangier lake and Scraggy lakes.
35	Frank Cope.	Hunting lake, Governor's lake, and Ten Mile lake.
36	Peter Joe Cope.	Fifteen Mile lake, Rocky lake.
37	Michael Tom (Toney).	Moser river.
38	Young Peter Joe Cope.	Large district north of Sheet harbor.

NUMBER ON MAP	NAME OF PROPRIETOR	DISTRICT
	SHUBENACADIE AND SHEET HARBOR BANDS—Continued	
39	Mathew Salome.	Big Liscomb lake.
40	Jim Paul.	Hunting lake and Liscomb river.
41	Abram Paul (son of No. 32).	Lake Mooin, back of Liscomb.
	CHEDABUCTO BAND	
42	Newell Denis.	Country harbor, Isaacs harbor, and north.
43	Steve Malone.	Loon lake.
44	Peter Anthony (half-breed).	Mill Village river, near Port Mulgrave.
	PARRSBORO BAND	
45	John Williams.	Shulie lake and river (Cumberland county).

SHEET HARBOR BAND		
46	Abram Gould.	Neighborhood of Sheet harbor. (He came originally from Cape Breton island, where his family had territory, and received a tract from the Cope family in Nova Scotia.)

In the nature of a correspondence with this it may be added that the same practice of charting territories and trails on rolls of birch-bark is a pronounced feature among the Montagnais. A number of such maps have been obtained by the writer for the Victoria Museum and the American Museum of Natural History.

A more precise example of one of the more definite hunting claims is furnished by the sketch on page 99 (fig. 3), which is a copy of a sketch-map made by John McEwan, of the Bear River band, showing the hunting territory of his maternal grandfather Siah (Sa''ya) around Mulgrave lake. There his lake and his river are shown, also the several stations or camps in the districts, marked with crosses, where he resided while hunting in the neighborhood. This specimen district is number 2 on Map I.[20]

HUNTING TERRITORIES IN CAPE BRETON ISLAND

The Micmac on the island of Cape Breton form now about the most conservative group

MICMAC HUNTING CAMP IN CAPE BRETON ISLAND

MICMAC HUNTING CAMP IN CAPE BRETON ISLAND

of this widely distributed tribe. Here, furthermore, is the seat of native government and the residence of the Grand Chief (*ktci·sa'ɤamau*) who has control of all the Micmac bands from Newfoundland to Nova Scotia and Quebec. The island of Cape Breton is called *Unama·'gi*[21] and the people style themselves *Uname·'wax*. They inhabit six fairly large settlements having a population of 604 in 1911; one, the capital of the Micmac, is at Eskasoni, where John Denys, the Grand Chief, lives; others are at Wycogamagh, Middle River, Malagawatch, and Chapel Island respectively, while the last, dating back only 50 years or so, is in the outskirts of Sydney. This interesting band still preserves its national existence and the records of its alliance with the Mohawk. The former intertribal negotiations with the Iroquois at Caughnawaga and the ceremonial procedures with wampum are still distinctly remembered.

According to the historical tradition of this band, it seems that before the middle of the eighteenth century the Micmac population of Cape Breton was inconsiderable.

After the close of the war between France and England for supremacy in Canada, the many Micmac who had been engaged on the side of the French, instead of returning directly to their former homes in Nova Scotia and New Brunswick, turned eastward and occupied new hunting territories in the sparsely settled island of Cape Breton. Here, too, they felt themselves to be farther away from possible vengeance of the English, who were settled in Nova Scotia. This movement was led by the chief, Tomah Denys of Cumberland county, Nova Scotia, who headed the Indians under the French at the battle of Quebec in 1759 and returned with them to Louisburg. Assuming this tradition to be fairly correct, as alleged by Chief John Denys, great-grandson of Tonah Denys, the hereditary successor to his office, it would appear that the hunting territories in the island must have suffered some minor alterations with the increase of the Micmac population subsequent to 1759. Such changes are, however, taking place slowly all the time, as territories change hands oftentimes with the death of proprietors. A knowledge of these districts through a continuous period of time would be very desirable to determine the nature of such changes as regard size and ownership. As may be seen by reference to the map, the territories are more numerous and more compact in the southern portion of the island, while in the northern and eastern extremities the family tracts are more extensive in area and fewer in number. This condition corresponds in general with the conditions in Newfoundland; by analogy, I am inclined to attribute it to comparative recency of occupancy. This is actually the case in Newfoundland. It must be recognized, nevertheless, that the Cape Breton band has been domiciled long enough in the island to have localized some episodes in the career of the culture-hero, Gluskap,[22] which is apparently not the case in Newfoundland.

After this historical digression let us proceed with the actual data concerning the hunting territories of the band. In Cape Breton the family claims are known as *nturəl'wɔ·'mι*. In practically all respects

FAMILY HUNTING TERRITORIES OF THE MICMAC OF CAPE BRETON ISLAND

NUMBER	NAME OF PROPRIETOR	FAMILY HUNTING DISTRICT	LOCALITY NAME
47	Newell Denys (*Nu'weli·dj*, "little Newell").	West bay, St Peter's channel, to Gut of Canso.	*Wi·a·'γadji·tek'*, "little place where red clay paint is found."
48	Matthew Morris (*Mu'lis*).	East bay and St Peter's channel to Salmon and Grand rivers.	*Muγala'γatc*, "narrow gorge."
49	*A'bslowes* (corruption of Ambroise).	East of preceding to Fourchu bay.	(?)
50	Louis Gabriel (*Lu'i'dji·dj*, "little Louis").	Trout brook to Gabalusk bay.	(*Ga'balusk'*, corruption of French "Cap Rouge."

51	Sam Denys, Joe Moose, Plans-way Moose.	Mira river and bay to Indian bay.	*Sula''γadck'*, "flat at the end of a gorge."
52	Tomah Denys (family with hereditary chieftainship).	East bay to Sydney river.	*T'wi'd'natck'*, "little channel."
53	John Isaac.	Sydney harbor to Little Bras d'Or.	*Kcatndcat'gade,* "rocky head."
54	Captain Francis, Bernard.[24]	South shore of St Andrew's channel.	*Ma'skwesu''γanikek,* "many little birches."
55	Michel Joe (*Mi'sel dŭ'dĭ'at'* "smart Michel").	Iona island.	(?)
56	Dennis.	River Denny basin westward.	(?)
57	Peter Kugu.	Wycogamagh bay to lake Ainslie.	*Wcγo'γamaγe,* "head of the lake."

FAMILY HUNTING TERRITORIES OF THE MICMAC OF CAPE BRETON ISLAND—Continued

NUMBER	NAME OF PROPRIETOR	FAMILY HUNTING DISTRICT	LOCALITY NAME
58	Paul.	Lake Ainslie north on coast of White capes.	Il'i'a·'γatck', "place where red clay paint is found."
59	Francis Newell.	Around Baddeck and Middle river.	Ebadek', "(river) dividing a hill in two."
60	John Kugu.	North river basin to Indian brook.	(?)
61	Charles and Ben Pollet.	Indian brook through Aspy river and bay.	Ktu'dwuk, "at the (north) mountain."
62	Common territory in band for fall berry-gathering.	St Ann's mountain and Boularderie island.	Muγula·'γadek', "gorge through the mountain."

their general characteristics are similar throughout the Micmac country. There was no clan, no regulation of exogamy, and no group totemism or social significance in names, so far as is remembered. The immediate members of the families constitute the groups having inherited or preempted districts for hunting, with the exclusive right to the districts as long as any of the sons of the proprietors are living to work them. Territories may also be transmitted by loan or through partnership. A point of detail, however, in connection with the territories of the Cape Breton band is the local naming of the districts. This does not appear prominently in the other provinces. Another feature of distinction is, perhaps, the occurrence of several fishing and berry-gathering districts.

Pl. xxxvii and xxxviii illustrate Micmac hunting camps. Several wigwams are needed to house the family groups; in this case two brothers were working together on their paternal territory. Owing to the scarcity of birch-bark, the wigwams have occasionally tar-paper coverings, although

the aboriginal form and architecture are
preserved   Pl. XXXIX–XLI illustrate details of wigwam construction.

As regards the Christian names of the proprietors of the fishing and hunting districts, it may seem strange to find them
so general; but this is due to early mission-
ary influence.   Indeed, as long ago as 1761,
we find mention of Micmac chiefs in New
Brunswick and Prince Edward island with
French names.[23]   In only a few cases do
native nicknames still persist.

In the table (pp. 110–112) are arranged
the proprietors' names and nicknames, where
they have them, their hunting districts, and
the native local names in the Cape Breton
dialect corresponding to the numbers on the
map.   On the map these districts are shown
as they were marked out by the descendants
of the proprietors themselves.   The Micmac settlements are also indicated.

HUNTING TERRITORIES IN PRINCE EDWARD ISLAND

Among the Micmac of Prince Edward
island, who are known as *Ebegwi'donax*,

BIRCH-BARK WIGWAM OF THE CAPE BRETON MICMAC

BIRCH-BARK WIGWAM OF THE CAPE BRETON MICMAC,
SHOWING FEATURE OF THE HOOP AND THE INSIDE
POLES FROM WHICH COOKING VESSELS ARE
SUSPENDED AND CLOTHES HUNG TO DRY

"People of the island in the sea," we encounter the same characteristics as those found in the territorial institution of the tribe on the mainland. The information which I give was obtained by Gabe Paul, a Malecite-Penobscot Indian of Oldtown, Maine, during a special trip to this band.

In recent years, it appears, the hunting has been growing worse on the island, the natives having had to resort more and more to fishing. An interesting legend accounts for the disappearance of the moose from the region many years ago. Owing to the small size of the island and the increasing population, the moose at first began to diminish. Then later the Indians planned a great round-up, and in a short time killed nearly all that were left, although some of the older people advised against the procedure. Consequently the remaining moose, offended at the thoughtless improvidence of the Indians, departed from the island, never to return. Some of the hunters claimed to have seen their footprints on the shore whence they made their escape by swimming.

FAMILY HUNTING TERRITORIES IN PRINCE EDWARD ISLAND

Number	Name of Proprietor	District
14	Bernard and Francis families.	Environs of Cascumpeque harbor, *Gasa'ngeg*, "bold landing place."
15	Piel Sark. (This family held the hereditary chieftaincy of the Prince Edward Island band. John Sark is the present chief.)[25]	Environs of Egmont bay.
16	Common sustenance territory of the band.	Environs of Richmond bay. (Here were famous oyster-beds, excellent hunting, and fishing free for the use of all the families.)
17	Mat Prosper.	Pannure island and environs of Cardigan bay.

From what can be learned about the methods of later years, it appears that the Prince Edward Island Indians had more communal hunting and fishing territory than is usual in the neighboring regions, and that fishing was relatively the more important activity.

Only a few family districts seem now to be remembered. They are as shown on page 116 (the numbers given correspond with those on Map II, Newfoundland and Prince Edward Island).

HUNTING TERRITORIES OF THE MICMAC-MONTAGNAIS OF NEWFOUNDLAND

Since the dispersion or extermination, whichever it might have been, of the Beothuk or Red Indians in Newfoundland, the Micmac have come to occupy the southern and western portions of the island. Here, in accordance with their custom on the mainland, the different family heads appropriated, for themselves and descendants, hunting districts which have continued, subject of course to some changes and redistributions, since the days of the first Micmac colonization. Incidentally, Montagnais hunters from Labrador, following the same easterly trend, have become thoroughly incorporated with the Micmac, so that, while the language in Newfoundland has remained Micmac, many ethnological and some physical characteristics, no doubt, such as they appear to observation, are largely Montagnais. In addition we have to recognize the possibility that some features of culture may have been absorbed from the Beothuk at various times, especially during the period when they and the Micmac occupied a village in common at St George's bay.

In studying the history of these Micmac-Montagnais, as we shall call them, in Newfoundland, we have some opportunity of observing the growth and extension of their family territories from their first foundation on the southwestern coasts. Assuming in general that this could hardly have preceded the arrival of the first white people in the seventeenth century, we can see, though only at a glance, through the period

INTERIOR OF WIGWAM OF CAPE BRETON MICMAC, SHOWING
SIZE AND PLACING OF POLES

PORT AUX BASQUES, NEAR CAPE RAY, NEWFOUNDLAND. TYPICAL SCENERY OF THE
SOUTHWESTERN COAST

From near here the Indians used to embark in crossing Cabot strait, to reach Cape Breton

of Micmac expansion and Beothuk decline, covering about 200 years, up to the present time.

The Newfoundland Indians, numbering about 300 by estimate, are known both to themselves and to the people of the mainland (Cape Breton) as *Taɣa'mkuɣewa'x*,[26] "people of the land across the water," the island itself being known as *Ta'ɣamkuk'*. The Montagnais proper call the Micmac *Aisï'me''uts*, "evil people." According to the tradition current among the Newfoundland Indians, the Micmac of the mainland had always some knowledge of the island through their own excursions by canoe. The route lay between Cape North (of Cape Breton) and Cape Ray on the southwestern coast of Newfoundland, a distance of sixty-five miles, land being dimly visible in fine weather. This bold journey was ordinarily accomplished in two days, they say. On the first day or night, if the weather favored, the voyagers made St Paul's island, *Tuɣwe''gan mɔni''guk'*, "temporary goal island,"[27] a distance of fifteen miles. From here three sturdy canoemen would paddle across the

remaining fifty miles of Cabot strait to
Cape Ray in Newfoundland.   Landing here,
they would await another calm night, then
build an immense beacon fire on the highlands to serve both as a signal for advance
and a guide for direction through the night.
At times even in summer the position of the
highlands is apt to be marked by the white of
snow-fields, resembling at a distance nothing more than a streak of cloud.   In clear
weather the elevated "barrens" of the Newfoundland coast show quite plainly from
Cape North.   The strait is often calmer at
night.   In this manner they made the
crossing, which is usually a dangerous one,
very rough and foggy.   In affirming the testimony regarding this difficult accomplishment, Frank Paul, of the St George's Bay
band, stated that the Indians occasionally,
even in more recent times, went across,
using bark canoes, in this way to Cape
Breton to participate in the celebration
of St Ann's day, July 26th, at Chapel island, at which time takes place the Micmac national festival.[28]   We may also
conclude that the Micmac migrations to

Newfoundland were aided considerably by French schooners plying across the gulf and Cabot strait. Indeed, the great-grand-father of Mathew Mitchell, who was a captain, or sub-chief, is said to have received a sloop as a present from the French king in order to facilitate the movements of the Micmac on the water in the interests of France. Then, as the numbers of the Micmac increased, their settlements were extended from the west coast to the southern coast and later into the interior. The first settlements were about St George's bay, *Noγwa'mkisk*, "where the sand is blown up by the wind." On the south coast the Micmac located at Burgeo, *Ma'γome'gwik*, "big fish river," and *Asiktci'gamuk*, "on the other side of the land (toward the sea)," now called Connel river. These and other villages on the northern coast, settled after the withdrawal of the Beothuk into the interior, will be found marked on the accompanying map.

In the St George's Bay region, supposedly near the present village of Stevensville, the Micmac remembers that his ancestors lived in at least one village in company with the

Beothuk, whom they term *Meɣwe"djik*, "red people." According to tradition, this amicable contact lasted until a quarrel occurred between a Micmac and a Beothuk boy over the killing of a tabooed animal, in which the Beothuk boy was killed. A fight promptly ensued between the two tribes on this account, and the Micmac drove the Beothuk into the interior. While we may recognize in this typical folktale a mere secondary explanation of the existing historical facts,[29] we can safely believe that it indicates an early period of contact between the Micmac and the Beothuk. This belief finds some support in the results of a study of Newfoundland Micmac material culture, showing a number of features peculiar to the island that are not attributable to the Micmac or to the Montagnais of the mainland, but which are thought, even by some of the Indians themselves, to have been borrowed from the Beothuk. We might infer this, for instance, for the Newfoundland type of canoe with the high-pointed middle, the boot-moccasins, and the habit of dyeing leather for articles of clothing a deep red, as well as a few other features which I have treated more fully in the preceding paper.[30]

Throughout Newfoundland the Indians refer to their predecessors as *Sa''ɤəwe᾿djki᾿k*, "the ancients," speaking of them as though they were the first inhabitants of the island.[31] Some of the older Micmac-Montagnais even claim that the *Sa''ɤəwe᾿djki᾿k* antedated the coming of the Beothuk. Ignoring such testimony, I think we may conclude that the term simply refers to the earlier Micmac colonists from the mainland, whose numbers were few and whose isolation rendered them distinct in some respects in culture and possibly in dialect. These people are believed to have been true Micmac and to have had a complete native nomenclature for the prominent places in the island. Some of the older Indians recall hearing about the last of these *Sa''ɤəwe᾿djki᾿k* in the person of an old blind woman who died in Sydney many years ago. Although over one-hundred years of age, she was conveyed in a canoe by her relatives, at her own request, over a large part of Newfoundland, giving the various lakes, rivers, and mountains their proper names according to the ancient terminology. In an appended note I present a list of some of these ancient names as remembered by John Paul, himself an old man. They are typical Micmac terms. The *Sa''γəwe'djki'k* families are said to have become completely merged with the later comers from Cape Breton and Labrador.

It would be interesting if we could form a more definite idea as to when the Micmac first reached Newfoundland. In the local historical records we encounter mention of them taking part in the troubles between the English and the French around the southn and ereastern coasts.[32] Other early authors speak of them. Chappell,[33] an Englishman, writing in 1818, says:

"During our war with America between the years 1775 and 1782, the Micmac Indians, inhabiting the island of Cape Breton and the parts adjacent, were amongst the numbers of our most inveterate enemies; but at length one of our military commanders having concluded an amicable treaty with them, he selected one of the most sagacious of their chiefs to negotiate a peace. . . . The old Indian ambassador succeeded . . . and received as his reward the grant of a sterile tract of land in St. Georges bay, Newfoundland, together with permission to transport as many of his countrymen as might be willing. . . . Accordingly the old Sachem left his native land, accompanied by a strong party . . . and boldly launching out to sea in their own crazy shallops or canoes, they eventually reached St. Georges bay in safety."

He also presents evidence that the Micmic frequently crossed over to Labrador from the south shore of the Gulf of St Lawrence. In the same book (p. 86) Chappell estimates the Indians at St George's bay at ninety-seven. The quotation given above bears only, of course, on the then more recent Micmac arrivals, as he was not sufficiently intimate with the Indians to have learned very much. His information, he even states, was gained while being paddled across the river in a canoe.

At the head of the Newfoundland band is a life chief, Reuben Morris, whose home is at Conne river. Although the Grand Chief at Eskasoni, Cape Breton, is higher in authority than the Newfoundland chief, this amounts to but little because the contact between the two bands is necessarily loose, owing to the difficulty of communication.

As regards Montagnais influences in Newfoundland, we learn that from early colonial times the Labrador Indians often traversed the ten miles of water in summer or the ice in winter, which separated them from the island, and established temporary headquarters there. Early intermarriages between them and the Micmac were so common that more than half of the older Indians in Newfoundland today have Montagnais among their grandparents.[34] There are now some families half Micmac and half Montagnais, besides a few true Montagnais, and to my knowledge, one Naskapi. I have made note of this in the tabular arrangement of the families and their hunting districts. Reliable oral testimony from John Paul shows that twenty-five years ago (1889) a band of Montagnais, consisting of forty families, from the south coast of Labrador, crossing the straits of Belle Isle, settled on the northwest coast of the island above Bonne bay. They stayed there hunting beaver all winter. Incidentally, it is averred, they drew all the beaver from that part of the country by leaving at their abandoned camp a split beaver leg bone fastened into a stick pointing northward. The effect of this magical operation was not counteracted until old Tom Joe, a Naskapi who understood Labrador conjurers' methods, threw the bone into the fire. When it burst, the direction in which the splinters flew denoted where the beaver were to be found.[35] Montagnais influences in Newfoundland ethnology appear largely in magical practices, while in material culture they are manifested in details of clothing, camp paraphernalia, and certain types of bone implements. It should be added, however, that some of the latter might just as well be attributed to the Eskimo, since they are common to both Eskimo and Montagnais.

Turning now to the proper subject of this paper, we observe at once from the map that the family hunting territories of the Newfoundland band are grouped in the southwestern portion of the island, leaving the northern and eastern tracts practically unappropriated. The claims situated along the western and southern coasts are the oldest, as evidenced by the names of their proprietors, who, we are told, were the pioneers of the Micmac migration. Farther inland the districts have been more recently appropriated by younger hunters, who have pushed into the interior. Indeed some of these have been so lately occupied that they are not well known among the older hunters There is, moreover, some confusion in the boundaries of these, due to still more recent changes among some of the younger men of the Paul, John, and Beaton families, who have taken up claims along the line of the railway opened some twenty-odd years ago. Under these circumstances, the fact should be emphasized that the territorial surveys, as I present them on the map, represent a combination of old conditions with those prevailing at the time of my visit. Since matters of this kind are by no means strictly static, we must allow for changes. These remarks apply likewise to other studies and papers dealing with this widespread topic. The local unclearness of boundaries here, it seems to me, illustrates the conditions which obtain on an ethnic frontier. The matter as a whole has, moreover, a certain significance in showing to what extent the frontier of an Indian habitat has expanded in, let us say, not much more than two hundred years of occupancy. In the last two generations of hunters, the tendency toward expansion among the Micmac-Montagnais has apparently been quickened by the absence of hostile neighbors, as the Beothuk might have been to them had they survived, and, at the same time, by very favorable game conditions. Nowhere in the east are the caribou more abundant. Several hundred thousand of the animals migrate semi-annually from the northern to the southern barrens and afford an abundant meat supply to the natives. Caspar Whitney has published a very interesting biographical study of the herd, the knowledge of which greatly helps us to understand local economic conditions. It will be seen, accordingly, by referring to the map, that the more recent claims in the interior are larger in the vicinity of Grand, Red Indian, and Gander lakes and Exploits river in the territories last vacated by the unfortunate Beothuk.

Regarding the hunting territories in Newfoundland, the usual Micmac characteristics stand forth, there being nothing particularly distinctive to note. The districts are termed *ntuaɣlwo'ˈmi*, "my hunting ground," the same as in the Cape Breton dialect. The families are fairly large. They form local groups, having more or less permanent headquarters in the different coast villages and in the hunting camps distributed through their territories. Some of the families now make their headquarters along the line of the railroad, where they can obtain other work when they so desire. The oldest hunter of each family is commonly regarded as the "boss." He directs the labor of the younger men, planning, from his knowledge of the conditions of the game, when and where they shall hunt. At his death his authority falls to the next most responsible elder of the family, whether he be his son, brother, or nephew. It sometimes happens that parts of claims are ceded as gifts to friends from outside, as an inducement to become members of the family either by marriage or by simple coöperation in the hunt. For example, Joe Julian, chief at Sydney, Cape Breton, was contemplating accepting the offer made to him by his friend Louis John in Newfoundland to share part of his claim at Long Harbor river (No. 4 on the map), where the territory was too large to be properly worked by the present John family. As might be expected under the pioneer conditions existing among the Newfoundland Indians, a rather weak sense of resentment prevails against trespass, which indeed can hardly be avoided occasionally, because the chase is concerned mainly with the caribou. On account of the absence of many important mammals from the fauna of Newfoundland, such as mink, sable, fisher, badger, wolverene, skunk, porcupine, raccoon, and woodchuck, hunting is practically restricted to caribou, bears, foxes, and beavers. Sealing and fishing are important to the Indians only while they are on the coast.

A few remarks pertaining to certain of the families and their territories are neces-

MICMAC-MONTAGNAIS FAMILIES AND THEIR HUNTING TERRITORIES IN
NEWFOUNDLAND

NUMBER	PROPRIETOR'S NAME	DISTRICT	FAMILY DERIVATION
1	Little Jim John.	Grandys brook and King George IV lake to high barrens near coast.	Micmac.
2	Paul Benoit (and sons).	White Bear river to Round pond, Bay du Nord.	French and Micmac.
3	George Jeddore.	Bay d'Espoir to Belle bay and inland.	Micmac, Montagnais, and Penobscot (?).[36]
4	Louis John.	About Long Harbor river north to Terra Nova river.	Montagnais and Micmac.

5	Louis Morris (hereditary chieftain).	Gander river to Gander lake and Gambo.	Micmac.
6	John Paul (originally Tom Joe).	Narrow strip from Hall's bay up Badger's brook into interior.	Montagnais and Micmac.
6a			
7	John Mathews.	Noel Paul's brook to Meelpaeg lake.	Micmac.
8	Frank Joe.	Sandy lake through Red Indian and Victoria lakes.	Montagnais, Naskapi, and Micmac.
9	Benj. Paul.	Deer lake through Grand lake to Lloyds pond.	Micmac and Montagnais.
10	John Stevens	Humber river to coast.	Mixed Montagnais.
11	Steven Stevens.	Humber river to Hall's bay.	Montagnais.

MICMAC-MONTAGNAIS FAMILIES AND THEIR HUNTING TERRITORIES IN NEWFOUNDLAND—Continued

NUMBER	PROPRIETOR'S NAME	DISTRICT	FAMILY DERIVATION
12	Beaton (family).	Recent general tracts about lower Exploits river.	Mixed Montagnais.
13	Mathew Mitchell (old chieftain family).	King George IV lake, elsewhere at will.	Montagnais and Micmac.

Note: The family and personal names in this band are often transposed; this causes some confusion to those who do not allow for this peculiarity.

sary. Regarding the claim held in the family of Mathew Mitchell (No. 13), the small size of this tract in comparison with the others is to be explained by the fact that the old Mitchell family holds an hereditary chieftaincy. On this account the Mitchells have the privilege of hunting almost anywhere without hindrance and even trapping inside of other claims if the proprietors themselves are not working at the time in the neighborhood. Consequently about the only place hunted continuously by them is around King George IV lake, as marked. Within the last twenty years Mathew Mitchell has hunted in the Bonne bay district, which had hitherto been unoccupied by the Micmac. Again, regarding territory No. 6 and 6a, held by John Paul in lieu of the original proprietor Andrew Joe's heirs, we strike a case of irregular tenure. This was the original claim of Tom Joe, at whose death it fell to his son Andrew Joe, who died leaving two sons who were too young to take care of themselves. Before his death Andrew turned the children over to his brother-in-law, John Paul, and left him a right to the territory under certain conditions. He told John Paul that he could take half of the claim for his own if he wished, including all the traps and camp property then on the grounds. He did not, however, leave John Paul the right to dispose of it, lest it pass out of the boys' hands entirely. Acquiescing in this far-sighted scheme, Paul left his own hereditary family district, took the southern half of Joe's claim, and now occupies it on shares with the two boys, who since reaching maturity have become his stepsons.

In conclusion, our information, when resolved to the proper perspective, leads to the opinion that, in continuous regions inhabited by branches of one tribe, the country where the family hunting territories are the largest is a country more recently occupied. The proportionate magnitude of the Newfoundland family claims is shown in the average of two thousand square miles to each, while in Cape Breton this average gives but four hundred square miles, and in Nova Scotia only about two hundred square miles to each family. Hence Nova

Scotia was doubtless the center of distribution of the southern and eastern Micmac, whose trend of migration has been continuously eastward. This is also conclusive from historical sources and also from ethnological considerations—rather satisfactory coincidences. I hope soon to try to determine the relative standing of the New Brunswick bands. After that the next problem to be considered is the relationship of the Micmac as a whole to the similarly distributed Montagnais north of the St Lawrence.

We also have information on the number and location of the Newfoundland Micmac from another recent source. Mr R. S. Dahl, in a letter to the writer dated June 6, 1912, from Placentia bay, Newfoundland, gives the following list of Micmac settlements and Micmac hunters which he obtained from Mr Howley. The settlements are: Conne River, Bay d'Espoir, about 125 souls; Bay St George; Codroy, one family; Bonne Bay; Hall's Bay; Gambo; Glenwood; and Port Blandford. In addition Mr Dahl gives a more complete list of the men inhabiting the Bay d'Espoir settlement. I may say that among these names are evidently those of some transients, recent arrivals, or of mixed-bloods, except for which the majority· correspond closely with the enumeration of the older families as previously given. The names are: Frank Joe, Little Frank Benoit, Paul Benoit, Frank Benoit, John Benoit, Johnny Benoit, Ben Benoit, Ned Pullet, Noel Louis, Frank McDonald, Noel Mathews, Martin and Michael Mathews, Noel Jeddore, Joe and Nicholas Jeddore, John Bernard, Stephen Bernard, John Stride, Reuben Lewis (chief), Peter and Micky John, John John 2d, Lewis John, John and Paddy Hinx, Mathew Burke, Len Joe, Ben Paul, Abraham Paul, Noel Paul, Matty Michel and son.

ANCIENT PLACE-NAMES IN NEWFOUNDLAND

On the Southwestern Coast:

Noγwa'mkisk, "place where the sand is blown up," inner St George's bay.

Kwes:wə'mkia, "sandy point," St George's bay.

Nudjo·'γαn "eel spearing place (?)," inside Sandy point.

Meski·'gtuwi·dən, "big channel," Stevensville, St George's bay.

Ma'xtɔgwek, "mouth of the river," Little river, on south coast.

Məski·gwi·'gante, "grass wigwam," coast between Burgeo and La Poile.

Ma'γɔme·gwik, "big fish river" (also given as "big swelling") (?).

In the Interior:

Ani·'apskwa·tc, "rocky mountains," south of Red Indian lake.

Meγwe·'djewa·gi, "red Indian country," Red Indian lake.

Mi·'lpe·g, "many bays." Meelpaeg lake.

Meγwe·za'xsi·t, "red-faced person," Hodge's mountain, northeast of Badger's brook. A local legend says that here was the last place where a Beothuk was seen.

Kespude'kəwi xɔ·'spem, "last lake," at head of Harry's river.

Ebɔgwu'nbe·g, "low bay lake," just east of Meelpaeg.

əlnudjibu·'dji·tc, "Indian brook," east of Crooked lake.

Medani·'ganik. "village half way," lake above Belle bay (Meddonnegonnix).

Xaxsxae·'gadi, "place of boards" (?), east of the last.

Kwe·'gudek, "on the top," above Meddonnegonnix.

Wendji·'gwamdji·tc, "little house," Wejegunjeesh lake.

Maligwe'djik, "low growth place," Molly-
gwajek lake on Terra Nova river.
Kepa'mkek, "sand-bar across channel," head
of Terra Nova river.

As might well be expected, some of these
names are of frequent occurrence in Micmac
toponomy. For instance, the third in the
above list, *nudjo''yən*, is given for two other
places in Rand's list of Micmac place-
names,[37] St Mary's bay in the St Lawrence,
and Chegogun harbor, near St Mary's bay.
No meaning, however, is assigned to it by
Rand. The seventh term, *ma'yəme'gwik*, is
also the name of St Croix river, New Brunswick (ibid., p. 43), and is given the same
meaning as in Newfoundland. The sixth
name in the list of interior place-names,
eb'əgwu'nbe'g, is recorded for Abegunbek
somewhere in Micmac territory (ibid., p. 12),
which Rand renders "a bending bay," and
the last two in the list above show recurrence
in Malegawaachk (*maligewe'lck*), a lake in
Ship harbor, Nova Scotia, and Kebamkeak,
the name of Bathurst harbor and Bathurst,
New Brunswick (ibid., p. 32), with the
same meaning as in Newfoundland.

APPENDIX

I—CORMACK'S OBSERVATIONS

Mr Howley, in his recent monograph on the Beothuk of Newfoundland,[38] does ethnology a distinct service by giving in full the journal of William E. Cormack, a philanthropic gentleman who, in 1822, undertook a trip in company with a Micmac Indian across the island in an endeavor to find some traces of the Beothuk. Cormack's work is entitled, "Narrative of a Journey Across the Island of Newfoundland in 1822." The author had something to say of the Micmac-Montagnais, whom he encountered in the interior, and his observations are decidedly worth quoting here to show how little the conditions of life among the Micmac and Montagnais have changed since then.

About half-way across the island Cormack and his guide, a Micmac named Joseph Sylvester, came upon the camp of a Mountaineer (Montagnais) from Labrador—

"who could speak a little of the Micmac language, his wife being a Micmac. . . .

He told us that he had come to Newfoundland, hearing that it was a better hunting country than his own, and that he was now on his way hunting from St. Georges Bay to the Bay of Despair to spend the winter with the Indians there. He had left St. Georges Bay two months and expected to be at the Bay of Despair in two weeks hence. This was his second year in Newfoundland."[39]

He had his hunting ground at Meelpegh lake, a body of water about nine or ten miles long.

"The Red Indians' country, or the waters which they frequented, we were told by the mountaineer, lay six or seven miles to the north of us, but at this season of the year these people were likely to be farther to the northward at the Great Lake of the Red Indians (Red Indian Lake); also that about two weeks before there was a party of Micmack hunting at the next large lake to the westward, about two days walk from us. He also described the nature of the country and made drawings upon sheets of birch rind of the lakes, rivers, mountains and woods that lay in the best route to St. Georges harbor."[40]

This Mountaineer was named James John.[41] A few days later Cormack met another band of hunters.

"They were Micmacks and natives of Newfoundland and expressed themselves glad to see
me in the middle of their country as the first
white man who had ever been here. They told
us that we might reach St. Georges Bay in about
ten days for they had left that place in the
middle of summer and had since been hunting in
the western interior . . . and that they
intended in a few weeks to repair to White Bear
Bay to spend the winter. . . . Here were
three families amounting to thirteen persons in
number. . . . In the woods around the
margin of this lake the Indians had lines of path
equal to eight or ten miles in extent, set with
wooden traps or dead-falls. . . . The Red
Indian country we were told was about ten or
fifteen miles northward of us. . . . All the
Indians in the island, exclusive of the Red
Indians, amount to nearly 150, dispersed in
bands commonly at the following places or districts: St. Georges Harbour and Great Cod Roy
river on the west coast; White Bear Bay, and the
Bay of Despair on the south coast; Clode Sound
in Bonavista Bay on the east; Ganda Bay on the
north coast, and occasionally at Bonne Bay and
the Bay of Islands on the northwest coast.
They are composed of Mickmacks, joined by
some of the mountaineer tribes from the Labrador and a few of the Abenakies from Canada.
There are twenty-seven or twenty-eight families
altogether, averaging five to each family and
five or six single men. They all follow the same
mode of life—hunting in the interior from the
middle of summer to the beginning of winter in
single families, or in two or three families to-

gether. They go from lake to lake hunting all over the country around one, before they proceed to the next. . . . A great division of the interior of Newfoundland is exclusively possessed and hunted over by Red Indians and is considered as their territory by the others. In former times, when the several tribes were upon an equality in respect of weapons, the Red Indians were considered invincible and frequently waged war upon the rest, until the latter got fire-arms put into their hands by the Europeans. . . . The tribes exclusive of the Red Indians have no chief in Newfoundland, but there are several individuals at St. Georges Bay to whom they all pay a deference. The Mickmacks although most of them born in this island consider Cape Breton, where the chiefs reside, as their headquarters. Their several tribes intermarry. . . .[42] One of the Mickmacks of this party named Paul, boasted of maternal descent from a French governor of Prince Edward Islands."

Further, Cormack says that ten days later he had the satisfaction of again encountering a camp of Micmac at what he inferred was the head of Little river, discharging from a lake which he names Wilson's lake.

"They were a party of Mickmack Indians. . . . Only one man belonged to this encampment. . . . This small party consisted of eight individuals, one man, four women and three children, one an infant. . . . This Indian's name he told me was Gabriel."[43]

A few days later Cormack reached St George's harbor, where he found shelter in the house of an Indian named Emanuel Gontgont.[44] These notes and the mention of family names with his estimates of population speak for themselves in comparison with what has been already presented.

II—ABSTRACT OF THE GLUSKAP
TRANSFORMER MYTH

The importance of geographical sites in a territorial study of this nature warrants the presentation of the following myth and landmarks, the locations of which are indicated by letters on the map of Cape Breton island. Each band of the Micmac seems inclined to localize the Gluskap myth, a comparative study of the versions of which will later prove interesting. (For this and other myths of the Cape Breton band the reader is referred to *Journal of American Folk-lore*, vol. XXVIII, no. CVII, Jan.–March, 1915, pp. 59–69.)

Gluskap's Journey

(The Cape Breton Local Version. Related by
Chief John Joe of Wycogamagh)

Gluskap was the god of the Micmac.
The great deity, *Ktcini''sxam*, made him out
of earth and then breathed on him. This
was at Cape North (*Kto'dnuk*, "at the
(north) mountain") (A), Cape Breton, on
the eastern side. Gluskap's home was at
Fairy Holes (*Gluska'be wi'gwo'm*, "Gluskap's
wigwam") (B).[45] Just in front of the caves
at this headland are three little islands in a
straight line, known as Ciboux islands (C):
these are the remains of Gluskap's canoe,
where he left it when it was broken. At
Plaster cove (*Two'bute*, "Looking out")
(D), two girls saw his canoe broken into
three pieces, and they laughed, making fun
of Gluskap. At this he told them that they
would remain forever where they are; and
today there are two rocks at Plaster cove
which are the remains of these girls. Next,
a little farther north, at Wreck cove (E),
Gluskap jumped from his canoe when it
foundered, lifting his moose-skin canoe-mat
out, and left it on the shore to dry. There

is still to be seen a space of about fifteen acres of bare ground where the mat lay. Then he went to Table Head(*Padalo''di'tck*) (F), on the south side of Great Bras d'Or. Here he had his dinner. Next he struck into Bras d'Or lake straight to Wycogamagh (G), on the western end, where at Indian island (*Wi''sik*, "Cabin"), he started a beaver and drove him out, following Bras d'Or lake to St Patrick's bay (H). At Middle river he killed a young beaver, whose bones are still to be seen there. Then Gluskap followed the beaver until he lost track of him for a while. He stood at *Wi''sik* (Indian island), and took a piece of rock and threw toward the place where he thought the beaver was. This rock is now Red island (*Pauyɔnuktc'gan*) (I). This started the beaver up, and he ran back through St Peter's channel and burrowed through underneath, which is the cause of the crooks and windings there now. Then the chase continued outside in the ocean, when the beaver struck out for the Bay of Fundy. Here at *Pli''gɑnk* ("Split place"), Split point, Gluskap dug out a channel with his paddle, forming Minas basin, Nova Scotia.[46] There he killed the beaver. Near here is a small island, which is the pot in which he cooked the beaver; another rock, near Pot Rock, is Gluskap's dog left behind at this time. Turtle (*Mi'ktcik*) was Gluskap's uncle. Here with his pot and dog he turned Turtle into a rock, and left them all there. Near where he killed the beaver are still to be seen the bones turned to rock. When he broke the channel in Minas basin to drain the water out, in order to uncover the beaver, he left it so that today the water all drains out at each tide, hence the Bay of Fundy tides. Then he crossed over eastward and came out at Pictou. While there he taught the Micmac how to make all their implements for hunting and fishing —bows, arrows, canoes, and the like. After a while he prepared to leave, and told the Indians: "I am going to leave you. I am going to a place where I can never be reached by a white man." Then he prophesied the coming of the Europeans and the baptism of the Micmac. Then he called his grandmother from Pictou, and a young man for his nephew, and departed, going to the other side of the North Pole with them. Again he said, "From now on, if there should ever be a war between you and any other people, I shall be back to help you." He is there now, busy making bows, arrows, and weapons in preparation for some day when the white man may assail the Micmac.

NOTES

1. R. H. Lowie, Primitive Society, New York, 1920.
2. There is nothing, so far as I am prepared as yet to say, in the somewhat classificatory kinship system of the tribe, to indicate necessarily exogamy or anything more complex than the loose family kinship formation which prevails today.
3. Father Chrestien Le Clercq, New Relation of Gaspasia . . . . Paris, 1691, reprinted in Publications of the Champlain Society, by W. F. Ganong Toronto, . . . 1910, p. 237 (original edition, p. 385).
4. Ibid., p. 235 (original edition, p. 380).
5. Ibid., p. 151.
6. Nicholas Denys, The Description and Natural History of the Coasts of North America . . . Paris, 1672, reprinted in Publications of the Champlain Society, by W. F. Ganong, Toronto, 1908, p. 426.
7. Le Clercq, op. cit., p. 235.

8. This practice is confirmed by Le Clercq (op. cit., p. 235): "The occupation of this chief was to assign the places for hunting *(de regler les lieux de chasse)."*

9. S. T. Rand asserts that the chief of the Cape Breton band was regarded as the head of the whole Micmac nation. (Cf. Micmac Place-names in the Maritime Provinces and Gaspe Peninsula, Recorded between 1852 and 1890 by Rev. S. T. Rand, collected and arranged by Lieut-Col. Wm. P. Anderson, *Geographic Board of Canada,* Ottawa, 1919, p. 45.) Rand gave the meaning of "Green boughs" to the name Eskasongnik (ibid., p. 27).

10. Anderson, idem., p. 45, note.

11. Le Clercq, op. cit., pp. 35, 38.

12. Ibid., p. 39, note.

13. By an acceptable interpretation the name Passamaquoddy means "Those whose occupation is pollock fishing."

14. The Malecite enjoy the sobriquet of "Musk-rats" among the Wabanaki, especially among those of St Francis, and the Micmac.

15. G. Mallery, Picture-writing of the American Indians, *Tenth Annual Report of the Bureau of Ethnology,* pp. 378–379.

16. Compare Speck, Game Totems Among the Northeastern Algonkians, *American Anthropologist,* n.s., vol. 19, no. 1, 1917.

17. J. V. Mays, Assistant Secretary of the Geographical Society of Philadelphia, correspondence with the writer, Jan. 24, 1916.

18. S. T. Rand, Legends of the Micmacs, 1894, Tale 21, p. 170.

19. Le Clercq, op. cit., p. 136 (in original edition, p. 153).

20. Since my talk with him, McEwan himself has written a short but interesting account of his early boyhood in which he speaks of being his uncle's hunting partner. Their camps were then on Smith's and Dish lakes. (Cf. Nova Scotia Guide's Prize Story, by John McEwan, *Forest and Stream*, October 1917, p. 466.)

21. This is an interesting name. It is regarded on good authority as a variation of *Mi'gama'gi*, "Land of the Micmac" (cf. Micmac Place-names, op. cit., p. 61).

22. In Appendix II of this paper is given an abstract of the Cape Breton version of the travels of Gluskap (cf. F. G. Speck, Some Micmac Tales from Cape Breton Island, *Journal of American Folk-lore*, vol. XXVIII, no. 107, 1915, pp. 59–69).

23. A captain is a sub-chief.

24. A Narrative of an Extraordinary Escape out of the Hands of the Indians in the Gulf of St. Lawrence, by Gamaliel Smethurst, London, 1774, reprinted by W. F. Ganong, *Collections of the New Brunswick Historical Society*, vol. 2, 1905, p. 380.

25. Through the kindness of Mr J. Robert Mutch, of Mount Herbert, P. E. I., this section of my paper was conveyed to the hands of Chief John Sark himself for revision after its completion. Mr Mutch reports Chief Sark as desiring to correct

the statement about his being hereditary chief of the Prince Edward Island band.

"Chief Sark's father, the late Chief Thomas Sark, died when Chief John Sark was a small boy, so the Micmacs elected Peter Bernard as acting chief until John was old enough to hold that office. Peter Bernard died before many years, and the Micmacs elected Joe Francis as acting chief. When John Sark became of the necessary age to hold the office of chief, Joe Francis would not resign. Mr James Yeo, M. P. P., had Joe Francis sworn in as 'Chief of Prince Edward Island Micmac Indians' before a Justice of the Peace, and had the papers sent to Ottawa. Another Indian belonging to the tribal council objected to Mr Francis being the chief for life and sent a protest to the Department of Indian Affairs at Ottawa, and they declared a general election to take place in 1897. Mr Sark was elected chief in that election, and the Department declared that hereafter an election must be held every three years. So that, while John Sark has been elected chief by acclamation at every election with the exception of one since 1897, he is not the hereditary chief, but holds the office by election." (Correspondence of Mr Mutch, May 10, 1920.)

26. In Micmac the character γ denotes the velar voiced spirant and χ the corresponding voiceless consonant. Ordinarily, too,

both *g* and *k* are pronounced somewhat posteriorly.

27. *Tuɤwe''gan* is explained as a place in some expanse which those who are crossing make for without knowing whether they will succeed; in short, an expected goal.

28. Another sea voyage of no little consequence which the Micmac were formerly accustomed to make was the trip from Cape North, Cape Breton, to the Magdalen islands, lying in the Gulf of St Lawrence about sixty miles to the northwest. The Magdalens derive their name from a Micmac woman who, according to a legend, was abandoned there. By means of fish and gulls' eggs she subsisted until her folks returned. I have recorded also a somewhat similar tale from the Malecite. While the theme of this story itself is an old native one, its particular application in this case is modern, a fact betrayed by the European name of the heroine. In an interesting and thorough discussion of the history and formation of the Magdalen group, J. M. Clarke quotes a passage from Brèard (*Journal du Corsaire Jean Doublet de Honfleur*, 1883), explaining how the islands were named after Madeleine, the wife of Francois Doublet, of Honfleur, who visited the islands and attempted to colonize them in 1663 (*Bulletin New York State Museum*, no. 149. Report of the Director, 1910; Observations on the Magdalen Islands, by J. M. Clarke, p. 139). An earlier notice

indicates that Indians were found among the inhabitants as far back as 1593 (ibid., p. 138). That the Indians also had concern with the Magdalens in 1721 is shown in a letter to Father Rasles written by M. de Vaudreuil (Jesuit Relations, Thwaites edition, vol. 67, p. 63–65). In this connection it may be added that several remarkable feats of navigation are claimed to have been accomplished by members of the Yarmouth band. Abram Toney, the late chief, is alleged to have been forced to pass a night on the whistling buoy twenty-one miles from Yarmouth, northwest, when overtaken by a sudden storm. Such things happen when the Indians are outside hunting porpoises. The same adventurer is said to have made the trip by canoe to Grand Manaan. Another Micmac with his wife and child is said to have crossed from Digby to St Johns, N. B.

29. A similar tale is recorded by Rand (Legends of the Micmacs, p. 200) to account for a war between the Micmac and the Iroquois. Cf. also J. D. Prince, Passamaquoddy Documents. *Annals of the New York Academy of Sciences*, vol. XI, no. 15, 1898, pp. 371–372.

30. See, part I of this volume: Studies of the Beothuk and Micmac of Newfoundland, p. 45 and table of comparisons.

31. Rand (Legends of the Micmacs, pp. 408, 432), also refers several times to the

"Sagawachkik" as "the ancients" figuring in Micmac tradition.

32. We also know that in 1765 Governor Palliser undertook measures to suppress Micmac migration from Cape Breton to Newfoundand, on account of the increase of these Indians along the southwestern coast of the island. (Cf. Chas. Pedley, History of Newfoundland, London, 1863, p. 121.)

33. Lieutenant Edward Chappell, R. N., Voyage of his Majesty's Ship Rosamond to Newfoundland and the Coast of Labrador, London, 1818, pp. 76–77.

34. Cormack, an explorer who crossed the island in 1822, mentions encountering an old Montagnais named James John (cf. p. 132, family no. 4), who was married to a Micmac woman in the interior. Later, in 1828, Cormack had a Montagnais, a Micmac, and an Abnaki with him as guides in his quest of Beothuk survivors.

35. Since then I was told some Montagnais once again attempted to lodge in Newfoundland, but the band was expelled by the authorities in order to protect the beaver.

36. Several Indian families trace descent from individuals said to have belonged to a tribe called *K̯n'i''bewa'tc*, living far to the west. Among the Micmac in general the term is applied to the Penobscot and the St Francis Abnaki. While the Micmac do not analyze it so, the term is evidently "Long River people" a synonym for the Kennebec (*Kʌun'i''bekʷ*),

River tribe of Maine, Penobscot or St Francis Abnaki.

37. William P. Anderson, Micmac Place Names, Recorded by S. T. Rand, Ottawa, 1919, p. 60.

38. J. P. Howley, The Beothucks or Red Indians, the Aboriginal Inhabitants of Newfoundland, Cambridge University Press, 1915, pp. 130-168.

39. Ibid., p. 148.

40. Ibid., p. 149.

41. Ibid., p. 150.

42. Ibid., pp. 151-152.

43. Ibid., p. 157.

44. Ibid., p. 159.

45. This is now known as Fairy Holes, between St Ann's bay and Great Bras d'Or. The Micmac tell how, sixty-eight years ago, five Indians—Joe Bernard, Francis Bernard, Clement Bernard, Joe Newell, and Tom Newell—entered the caves which honeycomb this headland, carrying seven torches. They walked as far as the torches would light them, about a mile and a half, found eight brooks in the caves, and when they came out discovered how a rock three hundred feet wide had moved since they had entered! The Indians naturally regard these caves as very mysterious.

46. The scene of the myth becomes changed to Nova Scotia, where the localities of the actions correspond more closely with those in the version of the Nova Scotia bands recorded by Rand.

INDEX

mac-Montagnais, 40; implements, Algonkian,
44. See *Caribou-antler*
Arctic zones, social life of tribes of, 84
Arrow, Beothuk sacrifice of, 62; in totemic
emblem, 96; *arrows* (Micmac), art of, taught
by Gluskap, 148
Asiktci'gamuk, Newfoundland, Micmac settle-
ment of, 121
Athabascan affinity with Beothuk, 71–72
Attleboro, Mass., Santu at, 58, 79
Awl, bone, Beothuk, 60; bone, Micmac-Mon-
tagnais, 39; iron, on Beothuk site, 21
Axes, iron, on Beothuk sites, 22

Bachofen, theories of, on social evolution, 84
Badger, absent from Newfoundland, 131
Badger's Brook, Beothuk remains at, 40, 48;
Beothuk site, 20; Beothuk tradition from, 53;
hunting charm at, 43; John Paul of, 27
Badger's brook, wigwam-pits along, 24–25
Bags, among Micmac-Montagnais, 39
Band, Indian, at Oldtown, Me., 115; *bands*
among Micmac, 92–93; Micmac, listed by
Cormack, 143–144; totemic emblems of,
95–98. See *Gens*
Bands, metal, on Beothuk sites, 21
Bank's pine, non-edible rind of, 77
Bark, canoes, Beothuk, 32–33, 43; receptacles,
Beothuk, 76; superstructure of winter
wigwams, 31–32, 73–74. See *Birch-bark*
Basketry, see *Splint basketry*
Baskets, Micmac-Montagnais, mainland origin
of, 41
Bathurst, Micmac name for, 140

AND MONOGRAPHS

25; clothing of, 43; foot-wear of, 35–36, 51, 75; wigwam lined with, 48; canoes, 60; capote of Newfoundland, 34; wool from, 37

Cartwright, Journal, cited, 73–75

Caughnawaga, Quebec, Iroquois of, 107

Caves, see *Fairy Holes*

Ceremonial simplicity of Beothuk, 15. See *Annual ceremony*

Chapel island, Micmac festival at, 120; Micmac settlement at, 107

Chappell, Edward, Voyage of H. M.'s Ship Rosamond, cited, 124–125, 155

Charms, among Micmac-Montagnais, 42–43

Charts, see *Maps*

Checkerwork design on caribou-skin coats, 34

Chegogun harbor, Micmac name for, 140

Chert chips on Beothuk sites, 21

Chief, Beothuk, wigwam of, 22; Micmac, bark map belonging to, 98; Micmac, gift of schooner to, 121; Micmac hunting territories distributed by, 88, 92, 150; of Newfoundland band, 125–126; *chiefs*, Micmac districts divided among, 94–95; Micmac, French names of, 114; Micmac, numerous family determining, 91; Micmac, of Cape Breton island, 94–95, 106–107, 125–126, 131, 144, 150. See *Grand chief*

Chieftaincies, Micmac, 94–95

Children, Beothuk, dyeing of, 63; Micmac-Montagnais, dress of, 35

Chippewan stock, reputed relation of Beothuk to, 71

Chips on Beothuk sites, 21, 24

Chisels, slate, pre-Algonkian, 13–14

Fences, caribou, Beothuk, 19–20; caribou, in Labrador, 73; deer, Beothuk, 46–47

Fire-arms, Beothuk fear of, 28, 47, 52, 144

Fire-place of Beothuk, 21, 24

Fires, see *Beacon fires; Forest fires*

Fish eggs, as food, 153

Fisher, absent from Newfoundland, 131

Fishermen, Beothuk forays on, 21

Fishing, districts, Micmac, 113, 117; implements, Micmac, 148; in Newfoundland, 131

Fish-spears of Micmac-Montagnais, 40–41

Flakes, see *Chips*

Flint chips on Beothuk sites, 21

Folklore, see *Legend*

Food, Beothuk, 21, 61–62

Forest fires, destruction of Beothuk fences by, 19–20

Fox, hunting of, in Newfoundland, 131

Framework of Beothuk canoe, 60

Francis, Joe, former chief of Prince Edward Island band, 152

French, blood in Micmac chief, 144; Micmac allies of, 108, 124; names of Micmac chiefs, 114; schooners, Micmac voyages on, 120–121

Fur, Beothuk garments lined with, 43

Gabriel, a Micmac encountered by Cormack, 144–145

Gambo, Micmac settlement at, 137

Games, of Beothuk, 62–63; of Micmac, 80

Game-totem, see *Use-totem*

Ganda Bay, Micmac band at, 143

Gander lake, hunting territories around, 129

Ganong, W. F., cited, 46, 74, 96, 149, 151

Garters, Micmac, weaving of, 37

Legend, of beaver, 126–127; of black weasel, 28; of Gluskap, 145–149; of Hodge's mountain, 48, 139; of Magdalen islands, 153; of moose, 115; of quarrel between Beothuk and Micmac, 122, 154. See *Traditions*

Leggings, Beothuk, 17

Leland, C. G., Algonquin Legends of New England, cited, 72–73

Lewis, Reuben, chief, at Bay d'Espoir, 138

Little river, Micmac camp on, 144–145

Lloyd, T. G. B., on Beothuk vocabulary, 67

Logs, winter wigwams of, 31–32, 73–74

Loin cloth, Beothuk, 17

Look-out tree at Red Indian point, 23, 78–79

Loom, Micmac, 37–38

Louis, Noel, at Bay d'Espoir, 138

Louisburg, retreat of French to, 108

Lowie, R. H., Primitive Society, cited, 83, 149

Lynx teeth as charms among Micmac-Montagnais, 43

McCloud, George, knowledge of, of Beothuk, 69

McDonald, Frank, at Bay d'Espoir, 138

McEwan, John, acknowledgment to, 94; Guide's Prize Story, cited, 151; map of hunting territory by, 99, 106

Magdalen islands, Micmac voyages to, 153

Magic, hunting, in Newfoundland, 126–127

Main river, see *St George's river*

Maine, aboriginal culture in, 13–15; Penobscot of, 15, 155–156; perforated stones in, 42; prehistoric Algonkian culture in, 71; wigwam-pits in, 31

Malagawatch, Micmac settlement at, 107

Micmac-Montagnais hunting territories in, 117–138; Micmac-Montagnais of, 25; 33–43, 86–87; Montagnais of, 16; tenure of hunting territories in, 109

Newfoundland band, see *Micmac-Montagnais*

Northeastern culture, implements characteristic of, 40

North Pole, Gluskap residing beyond, 149

Nova Scotia, Gluskap legend in, 147–149, 156; Micmac canoes of, 33; Micmac hunting territories in, 86–106; Micmac place-names in, 140; migration of Micmac from, 108; porcupine-quills exported from, 41–42; Santu in, 59, 65; size of hunting territory in, 136–137; traditions concerning Beothuk in, 71–72

Noγa'mkisk, Newfoundland, Micmac settlement of, 121

Nudjo'γn, village-site on St George's bay, 27

Ocher, see *Red ocher*

Ojibwa, hunting territory among, 85–87

Oldtown, Maine, Indian band at, 115

Orchard, W. C., Notes on Penobscot Houses, cited, 74

Osagäne'wi'ak, Penobscot term for Red Indians, 15–16

Osa'γan'ax, Micmac term for Beothuk or Montagnais, 16, 18, 56, 60, 65–67

Ottawa, ethnological collection in, 18–19

Otter, in totemic emblem, 97

Otter-skin, Beothuk clothing lined with, 43; wool from, 37

Pacifique, Father, on Micmac place-names, 95

Pack-straps, weaving of Micmac, 37

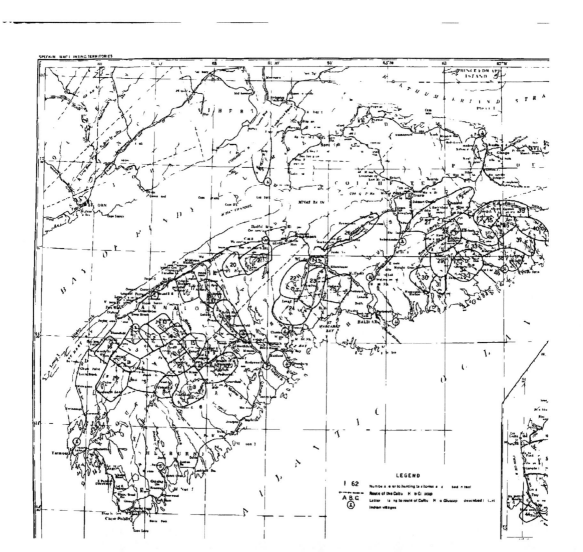

LEGEND

1 62   Numbe s e er to hunting te ritories a d   bed n text

————   Route of the Cultu   H o Gl scap

A B C
Ⓐ   Letter   la ng to route of Cultu   H o Gluscap   descended i t xt

          Indian villages

CPSIA information can be obtained at www.ICGtesting.com
Printed in the USA
LVOW112212120812

294035LV00004B/25/P